THE PIONEER ANOINTING

AWAKENING THE GENERATIONS
IGNITING CHANGE AGENTS
BLAZING NEW PATHS

THE PIONEER ANOINTING

BARBARA J. YODER

I especially want to thank my core leadership, who have stood with me, picked up areas of responsibility previously unknown to them, sacrificed their own comfort and ease, and cheered me on. I could not have written this book without them.

Core Leadership: Adewunmi and Ayo Gbogboade, Sharon Moore, Tommie Norman, Glenn and Jane Wilkerson, Eleanor Reynolds.

I am also grateful to all involved who have gone through this challenging period with me, standing by my side in supportive roles, family, friends, intercessors and staff. Only God knows the degree to which I am grateful for all of you from the bottom of my heart. I'm especially grateful to Steve Hansen, who assumed the role of media director and turned what could have been a disaster into a victory.

Finally, the following people have contributed significant stories, sections, and one person even wrote a whole chapter. I am grateful to them for their willing cooperation:

Apostle Damir Alic
Rhema Trayner
Michelle Hutchison
Esohe R. Osai
Jennifer LeClaire
MaryAlice Isleib
Tahira Reid
Elizabeth Doyle
Benjamin A. Deitrick
Justin Ford (a Facebook note)

Contents

Foreword

When we begin to follow the Lord, we are not following just for us but for all the generations that are to come. This is our call to pioneer and pave the way. Barbara Yoder has captured this all in her latest book, *The Pioneer Anointing!* In her previous book, *The Breaker Anointing*, Barbara shares how the breaker anointing is received when we understand that the Anointed One, the Messiah, has gone before us and broken the headship of our enemy. Those with the breaker anointing are those who walk in the ministry of a forerunner. The breaker anointing will break fear away from you as you move into the future. Tremendous warfare takes place at the gates, and only the breaker anointing can cause us to break through the demonic forces that control the entryway of our homes, territories, and nations. This is a season when God is anointing His people for breakthrough, and the pioneer anointing works with the breaker anointing to find a way for

God's presence to enter and bring true change into our lives, cities, and regions.

Throughout the Word of God, there were always people "pioneering" or paving the way for what was to come. As His people, we seem to continually be crossing over or going from one transition to another. Transition is a time of preparation. During this time of transition for the Church, God is preparing us to be victorious in the days ahead—to war for and rule our harvest fields. We must once again pioneer the fields and spheres the Lord has assigned us for harvest as we prepare those fields for the generations to come.

To *prepare* means "to make ready or get ready, to put together or compound, to formulate, to draft, to draw up, to frame, to ready for action, to gird, to brace, to fortify, or to strengthen." God believes strongly in preparation. In fact, the word *prepare* appears in nearly every book of the Old Testament. Throughout the Bible, we find the Lord urging His children to be a people prepared for what He has called us to do. God will use the time of preparation to release provisions to help us face the war ahead and accelerate His purposes on the earth.

Many pioneers have gone before us, met the Lord, and divinely linked heaven and earth. I call the spots where that has happened "thin places." These are locations in the physical realm where heaven and earth have touched as the result of man responding to God's sovereign call and will. These places can be small or wide and spacious, and at times, can cover an entire city or nation. When the Garden began, man connected heaven and earth, but man can also lose that connection, and the place where God has come down will then close. I believe our role now is for a divine return to the thin places. I also believe the Lord is calling His people to break open places in the cosmos of the earth realm that have never broken open. Only a divine connection between heaven and earth can cause the will of heaven to permeate the earth realm. In this season, we must learn our land and how it is holding iniquities, then engage the heavens until the very Throne Room of God comes to dwell on earth as we walk upon it.

The Pioneer Anointing is a must to help us pioneer again, break through and past our enemies, and align heaven and earth so those that follow can harvest the fields.

Dr. Chuck D. Pierce
President of *Glory of Zion International,*
Kingdom Harvest Alliance

Preface

Over three years ago, I was unexpectedly thrust into pioneering a new chapter of an existing organization. Truthfully, I never envisioned stepping into such a role at this stage of my life. Yet, the call from God was undeniable, clear, weighty, and inescapable. This book is the outflow of that journey: one of reimagining, pioneering, and bringing to life an organization shaped not by human ambition but by the divine blueprint God entrusted to me. In many ways, it felt like a resurrection from the ashes, a testament to the words of the Bethel Music song *Raise a Hallejuah*: "Up from the ashes, hope will arise. Death is defeated; the KING is alive!"

Just as it was with me, there is a call upon every generation to rise—to awaken to its purpose and ignite transformation in the world. Some answer this call with boldness, forging new paths where none had existed. These are the pioneers, those anointed to step beyond the boundaries of the known, to challenge limitations, and to usher in change that shapes the future. Furthermore, because of crises within each generation, there are strategic, opportune moments where change *must* happen, or cultural and spiritual deterioration begins to occur. If left uncorrected, the result will be devastating.

This book, written for this moment in time, is about the Pioneer Anointing, a mantle carried by those who refuse to settle, those who recognize that the shifting of an era requires fresh vision, unwavering faith, and the courage to lead when others hesitate. In every age and era, God raises up change agents who disrupt complacency, awaken dormant potential, and set new standards for what is possible. These pioneers are not confined by tradition; they are fueled by a divine mandate to move forward, even when the path is uncertain. And they unite with the generations before and after them, knowing that we must go *together*.

Awakening the generations is not just about remembering those who have gone before us; it is about stepping into our own pioneering assignment. The pioneers of the past broke through impossible barriers, roadblocks, and obstacles, but the work is not finished. Every generation has its own mountains to move, territories to claim, and revolutions to ignite—including the igniting of other change agents.

Igniting change agents requires more than inspiration; it demands action. This book is an invitation for those who feel the stirrings of something greater, those who sense the urgency of this moment in history. Whether sparking revival, launching fresh leadership, revamping culture, or personal transformation, pioneers are needed now more than ever. We are at a crisis point in history. If you feel drawn to blazing new trails, influencing your sphere, or birthing something that has never been seen before, this book is for you. (And even if you aren't, you need to be praying for these pioneers because the world needs them!)

Blazing new paths is costly, requiring perseverance, resilience, sacrifice, and great childlike faith that believes in the unseen. Yet, history belongs to those who dare to move forward, refuse to be bound by the past, and carry the fire of God's divine purpose.

Throughout this book, you'll see contributions from other pioneers called "pioneer stories." You'll find these excerpts in between chapters, taking what you're reading and applying it to a real-life story. These men and women have counted the cost and are true change agents in their sphere, and I wanted to highlight them for walking in the Pioneer Anointing.

My prayer is that as you read these pages, either something awakens within you or that "something" ignites, and you run to the call. I pray that the embers of pioneering faith begin to burn, that you are emboldened to step into the unknown, and that you embrace the call to lead, innovate, and establish something new. The time of transition is here. The changing of the guard is upon us. And pioneers anointed, awakened, and ignited are rising.

Welcome to the journey.

Introduction

There are pivotal moments in history when the familiar suddenly feels outdated, even irrelevant. Events unfold, innovations emerge, and social structures evolve—often imperceptibly at first. Economic and political currents shift, values realign, and everything quietly gathers momentum. Then, a tipping point is reached —a moment of crisis, a juncture where everything seems to change at once.

We are standing at one of those moments now.

These shifts are always challenging. They create a sense of social dysphoria, temporarily alienating many as they struggle to adapt. The Church, often lagging behind, may either remain unaware of these changes, maintain the status quo, or take an adversarial stance against them. Relational conflict inevitably arises as profoundly different historical contexts have shaped each generation. Their varied experiences lead to divergent perspectives, creating tensions that can feel like the old against the young, the poor against the rich, or the intellectual against the uninformed. Ethnic and racial groups clash, while economic and social realities further divide us, sparking battles among different social factions.

Even here, in the trenches of turmoil, God calls us to step out of our comfort zones. He challenges us to understand and embrace the new, to become leaders who embody and release the Kingdom of God—its realities, values, and hope —into the heart of these critical times and people.

Extreme historic shifts often feel dark, hopeless, and even apocalyptic. For many Christians, these times are inter-preted as the end—whether through the "rapture" that removes them from this world or annihilation by some catastrophic event, such as a nuclear bomb. The atmosphere feels heavy, foreboding, and thick with fear. This hopeless view of the future pervades many hearts and minds as many people think and expect the worst of scenarios, particularly the older generation.

Yet, in the midst of the darkness, God is at work. He is bringing His Church to the end of itself—a place of despera-tion, where hearts cry out for a fresh move of God, a "revival." Faith is at an all-time low. Bible reading has nearly vanished. The Church has lowered its expectations, focusing merely on producing "nice" or "happy" people while rejecting a theology that embraces suffering. Morality has eroded, and the Church often appears irrelevant.

The younger generation sees this and responds in ways that, though challenging or aggravating to the older generation, reflect a cry for something real, something transformational. Behind the scenes, God is orchestrating a divine breaking point—a moment of profound need and surrender. It is in this desperation that true revival is born.

This isn't new. Consider Romans 8:22–25:

All around us we observe a pregnant creation. The difficult times of pain throughout the world are simply birth pangs. But it's not only around us; it's within us. The Spirit of God is arousing us within. We're also feeling the birth pangs. These sterile and barren bodies of ours are yearning for full deliverance. That is why waiting does not diminish us, any more than waiting diminishes a pregnant mother. We are enlarged in the waiting. We, of course, don't see what is enlarging us. But the longer we wait, the larger we become, and the more joyful our expectancy. (MSG)

This is how the New Testament Church of Acts began, and it has been the pattern of nearly every revival since. When societal disintegration leads to pain, grief, and desperation, God impregnates us to birth something new. As He declares in Isaiah 43:19: *"Behold, I am doing a new thing."*

Considering what I've already said, we find ourselves in a time of profound spiritual crisis. We are living in a time much like the First and Second Great Awakenings. The world feels dark, and hope often seems elusive. Many in the older generation lament that we're "going to hell in a handbasket," while much of the younger generation *appears* disinterested—yet beneath the surface, they are searching. They long for something real: a fervent faith that is relevant, relational, and life-changing. God is inviting both generations into a new reality. Or, perhaps, it's a restored reality.

Meanwhile, spiritual leaders and intercessors are on their knees, travailing for something new as Isaiah prophesied. This "new" is both deeply personal and profoundly societal. It is revival within the Church—a rekindling of faith and passion—and an awakening that spills over into society, sparking reformation. This new reality will emerge like a fire, burning with the zeal of God, reforming what is broken into what is righteous and just.

These times call for pioneers—those bold enough to risk everything because they have been apprehended by God's call and purpose. They are the ones God has inducted to forge a new path, lead people back to Him, and transform irrelevant structures while driving the changes needed to realign a people—even a *nation*—back to God. They are willing to risk everything to see the purposes of God first in the area that they are called to, embracing the cost, which always involves persecution and suffering of some nature.

This is what God says, the God who builds a road right through the ocean, who carves a path through pounding waves, The God who summons horses and chariots and armies—they lie down and then can't get up; they're snuffed out like so many candles:

'Forget about what's happened; don't keep going over old history. Be alert, be present. I'm about to do something brand-new. It's bursting out! Don't you see it? There it is! I'm making a road through the desert, rivers in the badlands. Wild animals

will say "Thank you!" —the coyotes and the buzzards—Because
I provided water in the desert, rivers through the sun-baked
earth, Drinking water for the people I chose, the people I made
especially for myself, a people custom-made to praise me."
(Isaiah 43:16–21 MSG)

So let me ask you: What is burning in *your* heart as you
read these words? Do you have a dream or vision you come
back to time and time again? Whatever that "thing" is, even
if you don't know quite what it is yet, this book is for you. I
want to challenge you to step up and into a new place, one
where you're striking out on an all-new path. You were
created for this day.

Think of Nehemiah, who risked everything to return to
Jerusalem to rebuild the wall. He left the king's palace, a
place of certainty, comfort, and enormous resources because
he burned with God's vision to restore the ruins. He had
heard God's call and responded. Whatever is holding you
back, let it go and risk everything. It will be worth it.

This is your book and your day. God is daring you to step
into the unknown, to see Him miraculously go before you
and help you accomplish His dream for you.

Chapter 1

A Compelling Vision

W hen I started writing this book, I did not have a personal, compelling vision from God about it. What I mean is a divinely ordained vision, something that one actually "sees" while in the Word, praying, worshiping, or even going about ordinary daily activities. No, that was to come later for me. I began writing out of a "knowing." In my spirit, I knew we were on the cusp of an era that could—and almost certainly *would*—seem extreme regarding the degree of change it required. God was calling forth a fresh group of followers to forge a new path into the unknown.

A compelling vision is clear, profound, and directive. It is a force that ignites the soul and propels you into action. It isn't a dream or a vague awareness; rather, it's a detailed picture of a desired future. The vision feels tangible, real enough to touch. It can be described in every detail, including colors, shapes, imagery, and even movement. It's as if it can be stepped into.

With that vision and picture is an associated clarion call, a voice of purpose, clarity, and, at times, even urgency. It speaks louder than any doubt or fear. This call whispers encouragement in quiet moments, at other times roaring with conviction in the face of resistance. It's filled with the sound of possibility and hope, uniting one's innermost aspirations.

Jeremiah declared that the Word was like a hammer (Jeremiah 23:29) or a fire shut up in his bones (Jeremiah 20:9). It's an energy that can't be contained, awakening passion and determination and igniting life by aligning with something greater than ourselves. It's both exhilarating and daunting. It makes you feel like you are standing on the edge of something vast and transformative and being called to step forward. It can feel like a gentle pull or an unrelenting shove compelling you toward action.

A significant vision reforms and transforms the individual, giving them focus, clarity, and courage to overcome every challenge. It creates a compass, guiding decisions and aligning actions with our deepest longings. It calls out the best, the highest, and the divine within, requiring growth, perseverance, and sacrifice. It lifts the eyes beyond limitations. It inspires others to join, ultimately creating momentum and unifying a singular purpose with multiplied others.

You can't stay the same once you catch a vision like this. It disrupts comfort zones, awakens dreams, and kick-starts a drive that won't let you stop until the vision is fully understood and realized. It's a divine directive from God, demanding to be pursued. And the pursuit is for the accomplishment of something far more significant than you; it's for the transformation of others.

The Father and the King

So what about *my* compelling vision? I had already started writing this book, knowing it was an assignment from God. Four months and five chapters later, I experienced a definitive vision that had everything to do with writing this book. However, when I received the vision, I did not immediately understand the magnitude of it. I thought I was simply going to a prayer meeting that I was leading. We were going to pray for Croatia and the trip I was soon to embark on.

While in prayer that evening, a picture not unlike a famous painting flashed before me. It was very clear, with several distinct elements. Before me was this massive wheat field, radiant and shimmering with vibrancy. The gleaming color of the wheat field looked like gold itself. It held the promise of abundance, prosperity, and a future filled with promise and expectancy—like the phrase, "the best is yet to come." It mirrored a masterpiece captured on a famous artist's canvas, full of weighty glory and beauty, urgently ready to be harvested. It was as if the painting was saying to me, "We are on the brink of something great."

In the upper right-hand section of the field was a person who resembled an "ancient man" dressed similarly to the figures in the famous Jean-Francois Millet painting, The Gleaners. I eventually saw the man as both fatherly and kingly. It was his field. The fact that the "ancient man" was both father and king was significant—He was *our* Father and King. The two together represented a benevolent leader: the King had a heart for the people. God is injecting Himself into this new era with both compassion and transparent leadership for those who receive Him as such. He is ultimately the supreme ruler; there is no other. He rules the Kingdom. And He will lead us forth as a Father and a King.

This field belonged to the ancient man, but there was more to the picture. The man was bent over harvesting the wheat with a sickle in his hand. At the very edge of the field, the bottom left edge, there was the beginning of a new path being sculpted, even *chiseled* with precision through the field. There was no earthly comparison as I beheld the portion the Father-King cut. I could not even minimally determine what it was. The path at the bottom left resembled something an engineer designed, one who hired outstanding precision artists to carve out this path according to a precise, carefully laid out plan. As I looked at that portion, it was like I heard the Lord saying, "I'm turning the page." Then, immediately following that statement, there was great joy and rejoicing. It was as if every weight, concern, and anxiety about the future evaporated.

The newly formed path, finely chiseled at the bottom of the field, reminded me of the saying in *The Wizard of Oz*: "Follow the yellow brick road." Stay the course and trust the process. The enigmatic part of that picture was that the path was being formed by a sickle—the least precise instrument imaginable.

As I unpacked this vision, both individually and with others, it became clear over time that it extended far beyond the nation of Croatia. Croatia was the beginning—the starting point. It was the place where the vision was to be released first, and that in itself holds profound significance. It reveals a birthing anointing on the nation, a unique calling to initiate and pioneer. This vision was meant to create a new path, one that would take root and grow within Croatia. The nation served as the fertile ground, the spawning place where this movement would be birthed and set into motion.

Chapter 2

The Field

When we receive a vision, it must usually be interpreted—the more complex the vision, the greater the challenge of the interpretation process. Sometimes, I may not know fully what the vision is about until weeks, months, or even years later. As I prayed about this vision and began to interpret it, I suddenly realized it had everything to do with launching into the new, what we will see in this book as *pioneering*. It needed to be included! So, walk with me through what I have unpacked so far. I believe it will also give *you* vision for undertaking your new adventure into unknown territory.

There is a great promise before us. Throughout Scripture, we see God dangling a carrot in front of His people. However, he intends for us to reach out and grab hold of it! In other words, if we take action, there is something great ahead. Revelation 2–3 says to each of the seven churches, "If you overcome, you will inherit." There was both something to overcome and something specific to inherit. The vision I had of the Father-King and the path is about going somewhere we have never been before and the invitation to take the risk and forge ahead. So, leap with me into the interpretation.

What Is the Field?

When I received this vision, it was the Jewish month of Ellul. At first, it did not dawn on me that the timing was in concert with the Jewish calendar. The month of Ellul falls immediately before the Jewish civil new year, which usually happens sometime in the Gregorian month of September or early October. In fact, this timing didn't register until I arrived in Croatia, sitting in my hotel room a few days after arriving, spending some time with the Lord. I was pondering the vision when all of a sudden, it hit me: *This is the Jewish month of Ellul, meaning "the King is in the field."* I felt prompted in my spirit that this was not a month-long event like the Jewish calendar. It would continue throughout the new era.

So, what about the wheat field and its richness? Many believe that we are entering the greatest harvest of souls ever experienced—the billion-soul harvest. I, too, believe that, and I also see far more. We are in a massive harvest season where all hell has been and will be released to stop it. It involves not only souls but wealth, abundance, prosperity, fulfillment, and significant change. When I caught the vision, the brilliance of the wheat field astounded me. It was ready for harvest. It signified provision, multiplication (heads of grains are also seeds which, when planted, create multiplication), plenty of bread in the house, growth, and maturity.

But what might the field represent beyond the harvest of souls? It can be a place of assignment or operation, a specific physical location, a professional or academic area of expertise, or a symbolic area like a field of possibility or opportunity. For the new breed emerging—pioneers and creatives—it may be the field charged with inspiration and purpose, the arena of imagination and dreams for what can be.

Remember, when I received this vision, we were in Ellul, which means "God is in the field." Metaphorically, He has stepped out of heaven, so to speak, into our sphere of operation, assignment. That assignment is wherever God has placed us. In that field are souls, prosperity, abundance, and wealth. We are to identify the place of God's assignment in order to harvest the fullness of what He's placed in our hands. For instance, the apostle Paul's field encompassed both a geographical location and a specific people group. He was assigned to particular regions, and Gentiles were his focus. Peter's field, on the other hand, was primarily Jerusalem and the Jews.

Turning the Page

Change is obviously a significant part of the vision. Remember, I saw the very beginning of a new path being cut through the wheat field and heard God say in my spirit, "I'm turning the page." Change isn't for sissies. Change may require many things, like shifting relationships and alignments, moving geographically, shutting things down, exiting previous responsibilities, and discarding precious possessions associated with who you were and what you were doing. I believe that change will be huge because of how God phrased it. "Turning the page" symbolizes moving forward and leaving the past behind. It can signify starting a new chapter in life, sometimes even being a fresh start, transitioning from one phase to another, looking forward, and not looking back. It implies progress. All of these hold a sense of hope, expectation, and new opportunities. God is saying, "The best is yet to come," which is one of my favorite phrases.

Do Not Be Conformed

What about the sickle? Well, I received this vision just before I was traveling to Croatia to speak. Historically, Croatia was part of Yugoslavia, a communist nation. While discussing the vision with a close friend, she noted the sickle is often associated with Communism. Beyond its symbolism, a sickle is a cutting tool primarily used to clear weeds and overgrowth. However, it lacks precision, resulting in a rough and unevenly cut area after use. The path emerging at the bottom of the vision was remarkably precise, as if it had been crafted with the finest tools, resulting in an impeccably exact and refined trail. To continue crafting the new path, a new instrument was needed.

The fact that the sickle is often associated with Communism is important. What impact did Communism have on people that now requires an adjustment to craft a new path forward? For starters, it's important to note that it is you and I who are called to sculpt this path. In conversations with the Croatian pastors about the lasting effects of Communism on their people, they shared that individuals were conditioned to suppress their true thoughts, opinions, ideas, and innovations.

One pastor recounted how her father was imprisoned for an entire year simply for singing the Croatian national anthem in public. He did not do it to cause harm, create conflict, or disrupt the peace, but out of love for his country. He did nothing rebellious or evil. He simply sang the song he loved, which spoke of the country he loved. As a result of actions like this on the part of the government, many were afraid to even speak. They buried their thoughts, emotions, and passions. They learned to suppress their true selves out of fear of reprisal. They kept their ideas to themselves and shut their mouths. Unfortunately, once Communism was dismantled, they were still bound, as they had learned well to sit down and be quiet. It had become a well-crafted corporate neural pathway (more about neural pathways and neuroplasticity later).

Similarly, today, people are becoming bound by a "woke culture." For instance, they are becoming afraid of political, ethnic, racial, religious, and gender controversy. So, they either become argumentative or say nothing. They go "dumb." As I pondered the sickle in light of what it meant

for the Croatians (and us), I was reminded of Romans 12:2—
they needed a renewed mind.

The Amplified Classic Version states:

*Do not be conformed to this world (this age), [fashioned after
and adapted to its external, superficial customs], but be transformed (changed) by the [entire] renewal of your mind [by its
new ideals and its new attitude], so that you may prove [for
yourselves] what is the good and acceptable and perfect will of
God, even the thing which is good and acceptable and perfect [in
His sight for you].* (Romans 12:2 AMPC)

The Message Bible says it this way:

*Don't become so well-adjusted to your culture that you fit into it
without even thinking. Instead, fix your attention on God. You'll
be changed from the inside out. Readily recognize what he wants
from you, and quickly respond to it. Unlike the culture around
you, always dragging you down to its level of immaturity, God
brings the best out of you, develops well-formed maturity in you.*
(Romans 12:2 MSG)

Years ago, while studying this passage in Romans, I read
in one commentary that the word *world* could be interpreted
as race and ethnicity, age groups such as Boomers, Millenni-
als, Gen Z, or the generational age in which we live. The
generational age is the prevailing societal-wide culture of the
day. For instance, "ages" like the Agrarian, Industrial, Manu-
facturing, Machine, Information, and now the Digital Age

form diverse and unique mindsets. My father was a Caucasian man who was born and raised in the Machine Age in America. So his mindsets were culturally formed out of his race, which was Caucasian, and his generational age, the Machine Age, who were primarily builders who were consistent, grounded, hard workers and lovers of family and nation. Because of this, his mentality and paradigm were different from mine. Furthermore, it affected how he saw life and people and his attitudes, values, and norms. Did his paradigm line up with Scripture? Where did his mind need to be renewed?

So it is with me and you. For several years, I was at the forefront of racial reconciliation in the Detroit region. As a leader sculpting new patterns of relationships between White and Black people, I had to come face to face with where I had formed mindsets about race that were not in line with Scripture. I could not conform to the patterns of the "world" I had previously known, and my mind had to be renewed.

God did not create you or me to be diminished, cookie-cutter-like, "dumbed down," bound, or imprisoned with fear of reprisal because of our race, gender, nation or neighborhood, education, wealth level, or belief system. He designed us to be active participants in an epic journey of bringing heaven to earth, not bending to the negative part of culture we were born into or currently live in but transforming it. Creating this new path is a reflection of God's purpose for us on earth. However, this requires becoming a renewed people, fully operating with the mind of Christ—the Creator who designed the heavens and the earth. Because I am a Caucasian woman leader of a church and the Body of Christ, I have the opportunity and calling to pioneer a new path for both men and women, modeling the fact that this is possible to do without being gender sensitive for many other women. Many have let their gender, race, or generational mindsets determine what can and or should be. The significant issue is this: Are we yielding to the reality of our own life's formation or Scripture?

As 2 Corinthians 5:17 (AMPC) declares, *"Therefore if any person is [ingrafted] in Christ (the Messiah) he is a new creation (a new creature altogether); the old [previous moral and spiritual condition] has passed away. Behold, the fresh and new has come!"* This renewal calls us to reject systems that suppress our minds, creativity, freedom, and potential. To walk the new path, we must allow God to renew our minds and empower us to think, act, and create in alignment with His divine purpose.

Crisis is the Crucible for Change

We are at a critical juncture. God is calling us to co-labor with Him to bring about great change. This change is not just in and for the Church as we know it. It involves reshaping culture to reflect God's mind, heart, character, and purpose. Many credible prophetic voices have been saying this for years. I remember sitting at Glory of Zion Church in Corinth, Texas, where Dutch Sheets was speaking several years ago. I was riveted as he pronounced we were entering a "new era." What did that mean? What was it to look like? Who was going to do it? That kind of statement calls for both pioneers and creatives.

I love it when prophetic declarations intersect with current reality. God is letting us know it's time to shift, make changes, rethink things, and find a new path. Recently, I read a secular book by George Friedman called *The Storm Before the Calm*. It impacted me greatly and explained much of what we are currently facing as a society. The incredible realization I experienced was that he was saying what the prophets had been prophesying. What if the two sectors (prophetic and secular leaders) had actually been working together? They so complemented each other.

In *The Storm Before the Calm*, George Friedman purports that American history can be conceptualized as unfolding in two overlapping cycles: an 80- and a 50-year cycle, both nearing their end in the 2020s. One cycle, the 80-year one, reshapes the structure of government to meet the changing demands of society. The first 80-year cycle began with the American Revolution in 1776. Simultaneously, the 50-year cycle affects both social and economic realities (race, inflation, etc.). Both are intersecting simultaneously in the completion of their cycle. At the end of both cycles, a crisis erupts. The 80-year cycles have always begun and ended in war (American Revolution, Civil War, and WW2).

We are currently experiencing this crisis in both cycles, which has created a perfect storm of political, economic, and social upheaval. Intense tension and polarization mark the ending of 50-year cycles. Friedman sees these cycles of turbulence as a repetitive characteristic of American history. They signal the transition to a new era. With that transition, a sense of instability and uncertainty hangs over the nation. Friedman says that the nation always emerges with renewed and revitalized national unity. The crises cause pioneers and creatives to arise, creating new paths and structures. I personally think of it as an opportune time, a *kairos* moment. Crises invoke change. The nation has always emerged with transformed government and structures paving the way for the new.[1]

Moments of crisis always force creativity and pioneering action—often disruptive and shocking—to forge a path forward. Both Christian and secular disruptors with integrity are needed, ones not afraid of changing the status quo. The current era of seemingly insurmountable challenges is not the end. It's the crucible for the bold ideas and actions that will define the nation's next chapter. Call forth the pioneers and creatives!

It's Time

Before we move on, let's go back to where we started in Chapter 1: I needed a personal, compelling vision for the book you now hold in your hands. Through this vision, God informed me that the future is filled with hope. In fact, once I experienced and then decoded the vision, I felt totally expectant about the future. The current turmoil is not the

---

1. George Friedman, *The Storm Before the Calm*, Anchor Books, 2020

end but rather the stimulus to do whatever is necessary to harvest what is before us. A new path is unfolding. New leadership is emerging with fresh energy, vitality, and vision for the future. We are in a perfect storm not meant to destroy us but to initiate the new. It's time for the pioneers to step into the forefront, going forth in what God has gifted them to be and do. There will be opposition and pushback, even outright rejection. Nevertheless, God is calling us to step out of our comfort zone and leap with precision into the future, walking into the unknown together. The vision is compelling, the harvest is beyond imagination, and we are well able.

Pioneer Story: Damir Alic

Born and raised in Bosnia, a Muslim country, Christianity was not on my radar. As a young man, I completely rejected Jesus, even after hearing the radical testimony of a woman who witnessed to me. It was not only because of my Muslim background; it was also because I believed I already had everything I needed in life. There were things I valued deeply and did not want to give up. But one night, in a moment of surrender, I prayed: "Okay, God, if the gospel I'm reading is true, I want You in my life. But You have to do something about my situation right now."

That night, everything changed. God answered in a way I could not deny. Hatred and anger left my heart and were replaced by joy, peace, and love. My entire perspective shifted. All I wanted was God. Even when my father said he would publicly denounce me if I didn't leave this new faith, my heart still chose Jesus. It was the love of God that had transformed me. Nothing else mattered—not my business career, making money, or even the pursuit of personal enjoyment. By God's grace, I died to myself. And that same love and grace have sustained me through every trial.

You Have to Choose

As I sought more of God, I desired to be baptized in the Holy Spirit and walk in the gifts of the Spirit. However, my previous fellowship rejected me because they were influenced by denominational doctrine and negative opinions. Still, I knew I had to follow Jesus, even if it meant stepping away from the familiar. That wouldn't be the last time I had to be bold and walk away from what was comfortable. Later on, my "spiritual parents" offered me a leadership role in their group. The thing was, they required that I conform to practices they believed, and I did not believe some of those practices were grounded in Scripture. That realization was a test of my faithfulness. Was I going to be faithful to God and His Word? Or was I going to be faithful to people I deeply loved and respected? As painful as it was, I chose to be faithful to God.

Because I chose to be faithful to Him, I began to raise up a work of God, a church, in Croatia. Family persecution, financial struggles, and dealing with an unrighteous communist government were challenging. It was illegal to preach publicly or distribute tracts, and I faced penalties, interrogations, and even detentions that lasted multiple days. Yet even under threat, the group of people I led and I continued to witness boldly. Often, the same policemen who arrested us would later ask for prayer—for themselves or their families. I vividly remember one occasion when more than eight plainclothes officers raided a church meeting. They recorded all our information, and as the pastor, I was taken for questioning for hours. In the end, the chief officer himself asked me to pray for his family.

Division from Within

In spite of all the challenges, the work of God continued and slowly grew. However, the deepest wounds often came from *within* the Body of Christ. Misunderstandings and accusations from fellow believers were harder to bear than external persecution. Many in my country continue to resist the work of the Holy Spirit and speak against those who embrace it. Ministers who preach the fullness of God's Word are labeled heretics or worse. Even when private support exists, public support is often withheld. And this disunity among believers hinders us from the fullness of what God wants to do through His people in Croatia. People don't just resist the Spirit's work—they actively speak against it, creating division and undermining the ministers God is using.

Despite the division, God's mercy remains evident. The work has grown, and now we have a church that seats up to 500 people in the center of Zagreb, the capital city of Croatia. People are being saved, and new churches are being planted.

We have planted 15 different churches in various parts of Croatia and even extended our reach into Denmark. Recently, a new church was planted among the Gypsies in Denmark.

Pioneering Is Worth It

I believe there is so much more God desires to do as we, His Body, come together, laying down our differences—both with God and one another. Our God is more than able to accomplish this, but the question is: Will we align ourselves with His will and His ways? I am expectant about what God will accomplish through us if we do so. We have already seen miracle after miracle in raising up the church in Croatia and Denmark. Pioneering is very challenging. At times, it can be almost crushing. But the results—seeing people saved and transformed—make up for every difficulty that we face.

God Himself is on the move in Croatia.

Pastor Damir Alic
Apostolic Founder and Overseer, *Word of Life Church*
Zagreb, Croatia
www.tinyurl.com/46m4uphd

Chapter 3

Walk Off the Map

Recently, while half asleep and half awake (well, maybe more awake than asleep), I heard a short phrase: "Walk off the map." It was one of those phrases with that sound to it, you know, the ones that immediately make you think, *This is from God*. I knew this meant, "Don't ignore what you just heard."

I was trying to go to sleep, and the last thing I wanted to do was get up, crawl out of bed, and find a piece of paper and pen to write it down. Yet I knew not to ignore this phrase, lest I forget or minimize it. There was something big, unknown, even mysterious about this phrase, but I knew it was unequivocally important. I couldn't brush it off. I believed it was from God. And I believed it was a challenge to advance into the unknown.

Ignoring my internal resistance, I told Alexa to turn on the light, stumbled out of bed, found a piece of paper and pen, and wrote the phrase down. I sensed it might be directionally crucial for the days ahead, yet I had not the faintest clue what it meant or what its application would look like.

Walk off the map!

The next day, when fully awake, I began to ponder, mull over this phrase. I repeated it to myself, trying to analyze the phrase. *Does that mean falling off the edge of the earth, quitting standing, or stepping aside, or does it mean leaving the known route?* My mind went crazy with ideas, even wandering away to consider those who believe the earth is flat. If that were the case, I could just walk off the edge of the earth. Yet I knew that was absurd. And I did know that something about it meant leaving the "known."

As soon as my schedule allowed, I began exploring what this might mean. Unfortunately, there was no clear definition, so I had to formulate meanings from what I did read. Basically, "walking off the map" includes concepts or ideas such as "something that is no longer important or in existence." For instance, boundary changes could wipe something off the map.

Other inferences are leaving the known pathway, highway, or current trajectory or even stepping into obscurity. To walk off the map can also include seemingly absurd things like disappearing from known existence. Maps delineate cities, mountains, states, and lakes and rivers. If a river dries up, it disappears from the map. Apparently, this can also be applied to people who disappear from known identifiable existence. I've watched documentaries where people just vanish. Yet years later, they reappear as if nothing happened.

Other explanations suggest that falling off the map is to

leave a structure or a structured way. It can be venturing beyond familiar boundaries, exploring uncharted territories, or stepping outside of what is considered normal or a comfort zone. It's a new journey into the unknown. For example, we're living in a time where more and more people are leaving their jobs, selling their homes, buying some sort of RV, and then moving around from place to place like nomads. They're saving money, but more than that, they are free to move on from their location as quickly as they like.

The following are the three definitions that stood out most to me throughout the rest of my research:

1. To "walk off" something is to alleviate an injury, relieving the negative effects of an injury or condition. Sometimes, this looks more emotional than physical. We have to leave the known to leave an injury behind. For instance, sometimes someone loses something or someone dear to them, and the best option to free the "binding pain" is to leave the scene.

2. To depart very quickly or suddenly.

3. Some speak of "walking off "meaning to work off a meal by walking off calories. Weight can also be connected to other things, like mental and emotional pain that weigh heavily on us. So, to walk off weight could also be leaving unnecessary mental and emotional weight or baggage behind.

All of the above definitions contain nuggets or hints of

what I felt the Lord was showing me about this phrase. However, the bottom line is this: to walk off the map is to leave what you've known. When you walk off the map, what you previously knew or found comfort in is no longer important, or maybe the focus has shifted. In this day, God is asking us to walk off the map. Will you obey?

The New Era

In 2020, I distinctly remember listening to a nationally known leader saying, "We are in a brand-new era. We've never been here before." Something within me resonated deeply with that statement. The pronouncement was both huge and significant. With it came the sense that nothing would ever be the same again. *We have not been this way before.* And now, in this moment, I hear God saying it again. We have exited the last season to enter into the new one—the new era.

Most of the prophetic and apostolic voices have been saying we have entered a new era. The season has changed, and we are not where we were in God's timing. We must walk off the map because we are in a new era.

When God announces a new thing that redirects our path, we *must* shift with it. We may incur an "injury" attempting to continue moving forward if we go the same way we've been walking. Let me explain. The direction has changed, and if we fail to make the shift, we leave God's grace for the walk behind us. If we continue to move in the previous direction, He is no longer walking with us; His divine assistance is nowhere to be found. The failure to shift becomes treacherous to our peace and prosperity because we are no longer on the right road. This is often when some type of injury occurs to get us off the road we have been walking and motivate us to move in the new direction. It's off the map, off the path that we have known. To alleviate the pain, we must leave where we have been. Furthermore, a new assignment often initiates a location change. And sometimes, that change can occur very suddenly.

Early in my walk with God, I knew that God was speaking to me that it was time to move on to a new place. I loved my church, and I did not want to leave. I thought I could delay my departure to a time when I felt "ready" to leave, and I dragged my feet in responding to God. In actuality, it was rebellion. But I did not recognize it as that. I saw it as hesitancy. So, God allowed someone to "offend" me to refocus my direction. When I went to Him, murmuring about the offense, He basically responded that I had to feel it because I had not listened to Him directing me to change. I quickly realized that in His love, He allowed me to get hurt. Since I could not "hear" Him, I had to "feel" it. Once I followed His direction to walk off the map, the hurt left.

Let Go and Leave Behind

In addition to shifting and changing directions, walking off the map involves leaving weights behind. Once God's grace has lifted for a certain direction, activity, or assignment, what has previously been a joy suddenly seems heavy or burdensome, like swimming upstream, grievous, and lackluster. We are weighed down by what we try to uphold because "that's the way it's always been."

There may be relationships that were once vibrant and special. But now they don't seem to be life-giving; they have become a weight. It's time to shift relationships, yet we find ourselves resistant. I hate to break it to you, but the relationship must shift to move into the new. That does not mean we're going to drop the person. That's not covenant. It means we will shift them from a central place in our lives to a peripheral place. This is not easy, and we must shift with integrity, honoring what the relationship/person has meant and contributed to our lives. However, walking off the map means we must take a look at our relationships and make changes when necessary.

God challenged Abraham to "walk off the map" when He spoke the following to him:

Now [in Haran] the Lord said to Abram, Go for yourself [for your own advantage] away from your country, from your relatives and your father's house, to the land that I will show you. And I will make of you a great nation, and I will bless you [with abundant increase of favors] and make your name famous and distinguished, and you will be a blessing [dispensing good to others]. (Genesis 12:1–2 AMPC)

In Abraham's time, even as a nomadic people, they did not suddenly pick up and move. However, this move was crucial because history hinged on Abraham's decision. God was calling Abraham to step up to the plate to make a move that would ultimately lead to an entire people group he was called to be the father of. Abraham walked away from what "had been" to establish what God had called to be the birthplace and habitation for the Jewish people. He had to leave the known and travel off the beaten path, leaving his family and friends behind. Because of his response, a people group was formed, and history itself was set in motion. It was the beginning of something huge and, ultimately, world-transformative. That group is now the nation of Israel.

All because someone decided to walk off the map.

But Abraham was not the only Bible character who walked off the map and charted unknown territory. Let's take Ruth, for example. Ruth is one of my favorite books in the Bible. So many themes run throughout it! Ruth, the Moabite widowed daughter-in-law of Naomi, walked off the map. She left everything and everyone she knew for the unknown. All she knew was that she was to follow Naomi, a bitter widowed woman, and embrace her God, her people, and her land as if it were her own. From there, Ruth entered into a divine mystery that only God could have devised. She married a man named Boaz, and together, they birthed Obed, who was the next step in the genealogical path to Jesus's birth. Though she initially entered this family unit as a total outsider, she became the most intimate insider. She held the key to the future. What if Ruth had not embarked into the unknown?

In Acts 10, we find another example in both Peter and Cornelius. The apostle Peter was minding his own business.

He did not know a man by the name of Cornelius. In fact, even if he did, he would have avoided him because he was not "clean" according to Jewish laws. Cornelius was a Gentile seeking to know God on a deeper level. He regularly offered up prayer and gave alms. Because of that, God heard his cry and told him to seek out Peter to help him spiritually. Now, you need to know that in that time in history, Gentiles and Jews did not mix.

Clueless about any of this, Peter was in his time of prayer at the 6th hour. While in prayer, he received a vision concerning how he viewed what was clean and unclean, who he could visit with, and who he couldn't. God expanded his horizon in the vision, readying him to receive Cornelius's request. When asked to go to Cornelius the Gentile, Peter the Jew said yes. God opened his eyes and his horizon so that he could walk off the map, walk out of what he had known and believed, and what was prescribed as a Jew so that he could minister to a Gentile. Because Peter walked off his religious paradigm, Cornelius' household was brought into a whole new spiritual reality. They were baptized in the Holy Spirit and water, stepping into a deeper realm.

What about the 120 in the Upper Room? They heard Jesus command his followers to go to Jerusalem and wait for the promise of the Father. Thousands of people heard Jesus speak, experienced Him healing the sick and releasing miracles, and witnessed the demonized be freed. Of all those thousands, only 120 believed Jesus and went to Jerusalem to wait for the Father's promise. Only a few were willing to walk off the map. And they were his *followers*, not the crowd.

The Draw for More

Now that we've looked at a few pioneers from the Bible, let's look at a couple of real-life examples of somebody walking off the map. Have you heard of Rees Howells? He was a well-known leader, evangelist, world-renowned missionary, and intercessor. Multitudes followed him and became Christians when he did missions work in South Africa. After being in America for a season, he believed he was to return to Wales and start the Bible College of Wales. When he returned to Wales, he was so powerful in his delivery of the Word that multitudes followed him.

However, one day, Rees Howells walked off the map. He left his popular and powerful ministry both in South Africa and Wales to pray day and night for at least six years. (Let me clarify: He did not leave Wales, he left the renowned ministry behind.) God gave him a new assignment: to pray for England through WW2. He even mis-prophesied that England would win the war against Hitler and the Nazis in 1940. Of course, now we know that did not happen. However, that seeming mistake failed to stop him. It only helped propel him into God's destiny. Why? Because the crowds left believing he was a false prophet. With about 85 others, primarily college students in the Bible school, he led the way, praying England through to victory over Nazi Germany.

In the early 1900s, an African-American preacher and evangelist by the name of William Seymour stepped out of the cultural bias against him as a "colored man" to encounter the Lord in a life-changing way. Because of that encounter, he went on to birth the Azusa Street Revival. Before Azusa, Seymour had heard about Charles Parham experiencing the baptism in the Holy Spirit and was drawn in. He found out that Parham was in Houston teaching, and Seymour wanted to hear him. Seymour was not allowed to enter the room where Parham was teaching because he was not white, but he didn't let that get in the way. He asked Parham if he could leave the door ajar so that he could hear him. That day, he was baptized in the Holy Spirit and returned to California, not knowing he would birth the revival. What catapulted him into that place is that he dared to venture where no Black man was received. He did the unacceptable because of the drawing in his spirit to *more*.

We are now in a time when God is inviting many to do the same. He's inviting us into the *more* of something. It won't be comfortable, easy, or popular. It's a leap into the unknown. We probably won't know the ultimate results of walking off the map. Yet it's these "abandoned to God ones" who are going to become the birthers of the next thing God is doing. They will kick-start the critical elements of the emerging new era. They are the pioneers, the forerunners. They thrive in the midst of the unknown and move from crisis to crisis, miracle to miracle because they are willing to go where man has not gone before. They are the walkers off the map.

Are you one of them? Are you willing to go where it seems no man has gone before? I will admit that being a pioneer is like diving off a high dive into the deep end of a swimming pool and barely knowing how to swim. I remember when I was six years old, being led to the high dive at the end of the pier and jumping off. To this day, I can recall my heart racing—but I took the plunge anyway. At the time of this writing, two astronauts are stranded on the space station because they wanted to venture into the unknown and do the impossible. They thought it was about a week's commitment. Several months have now transpired, and they are still there. Not only are they still there, but every effort to bring them back to earth has failed. Yet they continue to see the delay as part of the adventure, leaving the known.[1]

In this new era, you have an amazing invitation from God to venture into the unknown. I can assure you you will be both scared and excited. Let your heart race and do it anyway.

Pioneer Story: Rhema Trayner

God called Abram out of everything he knew in order to go to a place that he would "show him" in Genesis 12. I know the feeling. Nearly a decade ago, God said to me, "I'm about to do a new thing in the Church, and I want you to be a part of it." He told me that I didn't understand it yet and hadn't seen it before. Suddenly, my "yes" thrust me into a new and strange tension between what was and what needed to be. I

---

1.   Associated Press. 2024. "NASA Decides to Keep 2 Stranded Astronauts in Space Until February." *Voice of America*, August 24, 2024. https://www.voanews.com/a/nasa-decides-to-keep-2-stranded-astronauts-in-space-until-february/7755711.html?utm=.

found myself gripped by an inescapable burden to go to a place I'd never been and see a thing I'd never seen. But what would it cost me to "see"? Would leaving everything behind even be worth it? I didn't see the relational agony, the mistakes, and the personal wilderness in front of me, but I quickly had to learn to redefine success as obedience.

God often births an answer to the thing you see *through* you. We typically have an invitation to become the answer to the very thing that disturbs us the most. This is what it means to *become the word*. We are meant to be bothered enough to cross a line into self-sacrificing love. You can only pioneer the hill you are willing to die on.

Where Are We Going?

I remember when I was first sharing our vision with others. I said, "I'm not exactly sure what this will look like, but we know God's leading us"." Most didn't understand. It wasn't a clear enough vision for the masses, but it's all we had. And looking back, it wasn't a call to the masses anyway. A pioneer never leads the masses at first. You only need a few who are willing to carve a new road. Not everyone is built for the pace, rapid change, and resilience required in those early days.

A few months into the first church we planted, I got a call from a girl from our team: "I just don't understand what we're doing!" she cried.

Through my own tears, I responded, "Yeah, I don't either."

For a long time, more people left than stayed—the revolving door of the pioneer's heart. There were moments when even I wanted to leave my church. (Well, it was at my house, so I had no choice but to stay anyway!) You lose many people along the way. And even though they can't come with you, you still have to go. Everything in me was increasingly dying, which I now realize was integral to the process. We are not ready for the path when we are called to forge it. We have to *become* the word that we're carrying. And when we arrive at the place we were meant to go, we're just as new as the thing we built.

We are trained to steward the small things and to hold everything lightly. I preached to no more than 25 adults for seven years. Once, I stood shaking under the power of The Holy Spirit as God told me that I was about to release "a word for the Church"—to 20 people who weren't all that interested. That word has become my life's message, and it's the central understanding of our movement, which now influences thousands.

You Have to Go First

God asked me at least three times to allow a version of the work to die, and he would take it and redefine it every time. This was highly problematic for a person who viewed an ending as a failure. But I had to learn that each season was a classroom, and I was gaining exactly what I needed for the whole journey. "The thing is not always the thing," He would say to me. Now, the blueprint I carry embodies the components of every season. Nothing was wasted.

You *see first*, you *go first*, and you *pay first*—and one day, things change. A new time emerges—suddenly needing what you've already prepared for. One friend told me, "You walk with a dim light in front of you, only seeing one step at a time, but you cast a floodlight behind you for those who follow." The pioneer walks the hard road so that others can one day travel the highway that cost you your life.

Rhema Trayner
Apostolic Leader of *Revive The Way*
www.rhematrayner.com

Chapter 4

We've Not Been This Way

This morning, I was sitting and thinking with God, meditating and inquiring. *How am I to proceed today? What follows the thought, "walk off the map"? How do I lay out this book in a way that makes sense? In a way that helps others find and follow the new, the unknown path, elusive as it may be?* Slowly finding its way into my consciousness was the thought, *Why is walking off the map important? I want to help people make the connection of walking off the map with real life.* The answer is actually quite simple: We have not been this way before. To walk off the map is to venture into the unknown. Into the new.

Now, my conviction is that everything must start with and be grounded in the Word. The Bible is our mooring point, our truth establisher, our pathfinder. It is God's very word given to us. In it is the will and the way of God. It not only establishes truth but also provides the paradigm for spiritually sound living and decision-making. It's important to grasp that the Bible is grounded in a Hebraic approach to life, which is both cyclical and ascending. Life advances in cycles that are repetitive yet progressively upward moving. This year, each Hebrew month reminds us of the same issues or focus as last year. Even though it sounds repetitive, it actually isn't because this year, we are progressing or moving higher in those cycles than we did last year. We are always advancing and ascending. Our life is continually more established and increasingly flourishing. Perhaps the following example may aid in understanding this concept.

I love sports and, historically, played several different ones for quite a few years. Tennis was one of them, and it taught me a life lesson I've never forgotten. When I was younger, I briefly played competitively. Through consistent playing (repetition and keeping at it) and practice (taking lessons to improve), I became more advanced. My life as a tennis player was cyclical, involving regularly occurring matches. Furthermore, I had to constantly take more lessons to become a better player. Lastly, I had to keep upgrading my tennis partners because I found I played to the level of my opponent.

So, what does this have to do with Hebraic thinking? Well, life is continuous and ongoing, yet repetitive. There are regular cycles of advancement based on certain principles, practice, interaction with a coach/teacher, and transitioning from playing with less-skilled to greater-skilled players. And so it is in the spiritual dimension.

Earlier in my walk with God, I would become aggravated with leaders who seemed to keep saying the same thing. I eventually came to realize that they were actually grounded in biblical principles of how we are to live. The same (or at least similar) challenges repeatedly cycle through our lives. However, if we are growing, that challenge is at a higher level. So it's the same but different. And because what seems like the same challenge becomes even more intense, we are forced to grow, to advance. If we engage in the conflict and persevere, we become victorious. There has been a repetitive theme in the past several years: the new. If I'm honest, I've thought a bit critically to myself: *How often do we have to hear this?*

The prophets have been driving us (at least me) crazy with the word *new*. God's doing a new thing. We're in a new era. We're graduating to a new place, a new position. We've never been this way before because it's new. Yet it seems that the same statement is never-ending. It's now sounding like the new is old! I, in my most unenlightened thinking, wondered when they were going to stop repeating themselves. Then, *bingo!* I realized God is constantly introducing and reintroducing us to timeless truths—the Hebraic way.

The Present Truth

Life with God is ever-evolving as we grow. We move from faith to faith, grace to grace, and glory to glory—meaning each segment should not be stagnant but growing, thriving, moving, and advancing. Even God's mercy is new every morning. What we knew of His mercy yesterday is old today.

There's a new aspect of His mercy we see day by day (Lamentations 3:23).

God is indeed doing a new thing, and we have certainly moved into a new era. However, we don't yet understand what the fullness of this new era is or means. We can see it now, yet we see it through a glass dimly. But it is a truth grounded in God's Word, as seen in the following verses in Isaiah.

"Behold, the former things have come to pass, and new things I now declare; before they spring forth I tell you of them." (Isaiah 42:9 AMPC)

"Behold, I am doing a new thing! Now it springs forth; do you not perceive and know it and will you not give heed to it? I will even make a way in the wilderness and rivers in the desert." (Isaiah 43:19 AMPC)

The apostle Peter also spoke to the issue of the ever-evolving understanding of God's truth in the following 2 Peter 1:12 (NKJV): *"For this reason I will not be negligent to remind you always of these things, though you know and are established in the present truth"*. In other words, we may know truth initially, but there is a more comprehensive revelatory grasping of its fullness that is to continually unfold. Most commentators interpret this verse to mean the current biblical revelation we possess.

Historically, we can recall moves of God that shed light on biblical truth we had been blinded to. For example, the

Azusa Street revival brought to light the Baptism in the Holy Spirit. The Faith Movement illuminated faith in a fresh way. The Prophetic Movement moved prophets and prophecy to the forefront, releasing fresh understanding and truth.

As a young person, even though I read the Bible, I seemed to be blinded to the truth of the Baptism in the Holy Spirit. I mean, I read it in the Bible because I read through the Bible. But I did not *see* this truth. It was like I read the passage in Acts, but it did not register. Similarly, I seemed to have stumbled over any passage that spoke of speaking or praying in tongues. However, once it became revealed truth to me, my life was instantly transformed. What was ages old biblically suddenly became a *present* truth, which caused it to become a reality in my life. It changed my whole paradigm, as well as my behavior.

We Haven't Seen Anything Yet!

Let's go back to the beginning of this chapter for a moment. What is it that causes me to say "We've not been this way before?" It's both the Bible truth and a prophetic forecasting statement of the time we are in. We are entering into a place we have never been before—a place we've only heard of and hoped for. Haggai 2:9 says, *"The glory of this latter temple shall be greater than the former"* (NKJV). We are coming into a time that, personally, I doubt we can even comprehend the greatness and magnificence of yet. We know the prophecies about such things as the billion-soul harvest, nations completely discipled and transformed—reformed, rather—

and cities aflame with the glory of God. We've heard about a body of believers who are similar yet greater than the first-century ones and an overwhelming reestablishment of the fear of the Lord. Leaders have even referenced the full restoration and placement of the five-fold ministry—apostles, prophets, evangelists, pastors, and teachers. Several have prophesied about the supernatural prosperity that will cloak the end-time restored church. Fascinatingly enough, Haggai 2 links the gold and silver with the latter temple.

But can we actually comprehend these prophetic words yet? Ordinary people will be clothed with both supernatural authority (*exousia*—a God-given legal right) and power (*dunamis*—God-given miraculous power and ability). Many of us have seen amazing miracles of healing and deliverance, but the bottom line is, "We haven't seen anything yet"!

Fullness of Time

So, we know that we're going where we've never gone before, and we know that it will be even greater than we could have ever asked or dreamed (Ephesians 3:20). But, what is it? Will we even know what "it" is? At the time of this writing, I posted a short blurb on Facebook that digs a little deeper into the place the pioneer likely finds themselves right now:

> *I believe that we are in a divine pause. Caught between what has been and what is about to unfold. That means we can't quite find what our heart is reaching out for, looking for. We can't quite find what or where the new is. We search for the "sound,"*

hear great words—sounds, yet none of them are the "sound"
we're listening for. It feels like we are in a type of limbo. (Limbo
—one phase of transition.) Something has ended and we can't
quite see or grasp the new beginning.

As pioneers, many of us are looking around to see if there's someone carrying the "message" that sets our hearts on fire. Yet no one seems to have that piece that finishes the puzzle. That doesn't mean that anybody is wrong or off. It simply means that the final piece hasn't yet been unveiled. We are entering the end-time Apostolic Age. The Kingdom Age. It has begun to trickle in, but it's only a dribble. And what we do see is not entirely it.

The Apostolic Age is that which was demonstrated by the New Testament church birthed on the day of Pentecost. To birth that movement, a critical mass of people required an overpowering encounter which both transformed and reformed them for the rolling out of the new.

Historically, there has always, at some point, been a "fullness of time." This happens when God releases both the revelation and action necessary to fully unveil and transition us into *His* fullness of time. It is marked by some sort of monumental event that captures our attention and spirit. In one overwhelming instant, we are changed. We are moved from the waiting room to the happening room. Until then, we are still waiting, positioned for the visible emergence of what's been being formed in secret. There is great anticipation and expectation. It only requires a few who see it, know it's coming, and will wait out the process, persevering to the breaking out event.

What do I mean? In January of 2019 or 2020, I was listening to Dutch Sheets at Glory of Zion Church in Corinth, Texas. There was a moment when Dutch suddenly moved from teaching to powerfully prophetically declaring that we were now entering a new era. I don't know quite how to put it into words except that I felt "slammed" or internally powerfully propelled into a new place. It was sudden and extreme, totally in the revelatory realm and not actual reality. It was as if one moment I didn't see it, then the next moment I saw it completely and it immediately changed my paradigm for the future. That moment became a fullness of time for me. Something had just ended, and I was at the threshold of the new, though I didn't know what it was.

The Suddenly Is Coming

In this season, we must learn to discern Holy Spirit's every nudge, every whisper, every movement, every command. For in His faithfulness, He will cause us to keep advancing until we find that new place; until we are visited from on high, overwhelmed and overtaken anew by the Holy Spirit, picked up and placed positionally and revelationally where we've never been before.

There is a new visitation of Acts 2 coming. We will very suddenly become a different people. We will have to walk off the map to get there—to go and do what we've never done before, leaving comfort and the "known" behind. It will take great faith and careful listening to and following the Holy Spirit. But it will be worth the trust and the cost. Selah!

Michelle Hutchison: Rewiring the Brain

The church, both as a collective group and as individuals making up the body of Christ, can often find ourselves unintentionally working against the very transition that God is bringing us into. And if we're not careful, we can do that very thing in the time we're living in. The historic shift we are entering into will require a greater spiritual sensitivity and partnership, as well as physiological mindset changes. It is both spiritual *and* practical. Acquiring a greater understanding and value of our humanity allows us to partner with what God is doing in the heart *and* mind, bringing about the transformation essential to transition.

We must understand that when we remain captured by beliefs of doom, hopelessness, and apocalyptic thinking, we inhibit the explosion of growth that God wants to bring us into, both personally and corporately. This is detrimental to the impact of the church within society. During this time of transition, we need to understand two important concepts as they relate to our thinking. First, we need to understand the concept of **neuroplasticity**, and second, we need to understand **resilience**. Gaining a greater understanding of our thought life does not negate the spiritual. Instead, it actually enhances our ability to partner with the Holy Spirit for more timely and significant outcomes.

Let's get started by tackling the topic of neuroplasticity.

Another Type of New Path

Neuroplasticity is the ability of the brain to grow and change. This growth can be understood as the renewing of the mind. This is not only a change in thinking; the renewing of the mind in its proper form brings a shift in the tangible structure of the brain, which then facilitates behavioral outcomes. See, the mind and the brain are not the same, although linguistically, we combine them. Our **brain** —the actual physical brain that a doctor can do surgery on —comprises cells that can be formed, reformed, damaged, or grown. The **mind** can be described as the place where we hold our thoughts, will, and emotions. These thoughts, while intangible, are made up of scientifically trackable cellular energy. This cellular energy sparks the firing of neurons and synapses, creating a tangible physical structure called the brain. The brain and the mind are different, yet interchangeably impact one another.

The more we experience a thought, the more we begin to believe that thought. Then, as we embrace a thought pattern, we grow and solidify deeper and wider neuropathways, creating the physiological structure of our brain. When this structuring occurs, our brain's default response will be the pathway of thinking and behavior that has been most reinforced. For example, if I always see the negative in situations, I will look for the negative in every situation. When I am sick and tired of seeing the negative around me, and I open my mind to looking for the good in every circumstance, I can develop a new outlook on life based on a new pattern of thinking. As this new structure builds, I will naturally see the good instead of the negative.

The beautiful truth of neuroplasticity is that we *can* change the very makeup of our thoughts and corresponding behaviors. See, if you will, our brains are lazy and prefer to take the easier course of action. Think of it like this: imagine that there's a path already paved in the snow; it is easier to walk this path than to begin a new one. Now, imagine you start to develop a new path in the snow. When building this new path, the more you use it, the clearer it becomes. When fresh snow begins falling and covering up the old path until it can no longer be seen, the new path has become the natural option.

This example mirrors our ability to restructure our brains by managing our thought lives. We will think and behave according to the old until we begin the practice of renewing our thought life. Our thoughts dictate our behaviors, and our behaviors dictate our outcomes. Once we practice changing our thought life, the old dies off, and we begin engaging the new. This process is a picture of what God is calling us to, in partnership with the Holy Spirit, in Romans 12:2. Understanding this process is a key to our partnering in humanity with the supernatural journey of moving from glory to glory.

The constant walk of renewal with the Holy Spirit will catapult us into the "new" instead of getting stuck in stagnant growth and experience. While you're practicing and learning this new way, ask the Holy Spirit to prompt you when you drift into old thinking. Then stop and consider what is happening in your thought life, and ask the Holy Spirit for a new perspective. Once you put this practice in place and are consistent, you will find a renewed outlook and a greater unfolding of walking out the spiritual call over your life.

Resilience: Not Just a Character Trait

Alright, next, let's talk about the concept of resilience. Resilience is built and strengthened through adversity and is, in short, the ability to "bounce back" after times of suffering. It's important to note that levels of resilience vary individually based on environmental factors, personality, brain structure, and learned coping mechanisms. Again, we're speaking of the physical brain here. A brain that is less resilient in the face of adversity may experience potential shriveling or weakening of the neurons, impacting one's thoughts and behaviors. Individuals with less resilience may experience a lack of coping mechanisms and motivation, tend to see themselves as victims, and may experience increased depression and anxiety. A more resilient brain structure allows an individual to rebound with growth, equating to an outlook of greater understanding, strength, cognition, spiritual fortitude, and remaining positive in the face of adversity moving forward.

Developing a resilient mind and a resilient church requires a mindset of renewed thinking wherein we, through faith, recognize that God is working all things together for the good and there is always hope. Faith allows us to see into the future and know the truth that we can trust God will bring fruitful outcomes. If we then bridge resilience with the renewing of our thoughts, we become individuals who look for God's outcomes and see all circumstances with hope and willingness to step into the unknown.

It's Time for the New!

So, what does this have to do with what God is doing in this new historic shift? Well, since God is asking us to do away with old mindsets in this hour, we have to take action to start to look at our world and our life circumstances through a different lens—the lens that is resilient and continually being renewed. He has to move us out of a place of doom and gloom thinking and into recognizing our role and responsibility to steward the Kingdom on earth, but this requires a new mindset. It requires the mind of Christ.

What is coming for the church is *not* doom and gloom. What is coming involves the belief for the church's prosperity in the face of adversity and understanding in the process of character reformation! Walking in belief, trust, and faith allows us to live in a mindset of authority, rest, joy, and peace, even in the unknown. We must stay alert for what he is teaching us in the new and partner with him in a way that motivates us to walk through adversity with hope. This new brain structure allows the church to throw away old thoughts and behavioral patterns such as fear, hopelessness, and apocalyptic thinking. Instead, we will be able to partner with the mind of Christ to see the the church as being in a place of individual and corporate renewal, ready for the power and authority He is about to release.

God is reforming our thought life to position His people to step into Kingdom mandates with greater understanding and partnership with the Holy Spirit, futuristic thinking, and greater sensitivity and belief in the supernatural. This will require surrendering our ways, positioning our thoughts, and a readiness to step into the bursting out of the brand-new, the unknown, with trust, hope, joy, and authority. I implore you to ask the Lord to show you old mindsets that he wants to purge and give you a new perspective. As he provides a new perspective, it is your responsibility to believe, to interrupt the old, and to practice the new thought.

It's time for the new!

Michelle Hutchison
LMSW Consultant and Speaker
Resilient Minds Consulting
Resilientmindsconsulting.com

Chapter 5

The Pregnant Void

We have not been this way before! To get there, we must walk off the map, the known path, to break through to the new. Often, it feels as if we are in some sort of limbo. We anticipate what is to come, yet we can't locate our current positioning or the way ahead. It's like the GPS in our car just drove us off the map. We know where we've come from and can't go back, and we neither know how to forge ahead because the GPS is now silent! We're hanging in the unknown between what was and what is to be. We know where we want to go but are lost in the process. Spiritually speaking, it's as if God has quit talking to us.

Though this is unfamiliar territory, we can discover similar conundrums in Scripture. I believe there is always a pattern in Scripture that sheds light on our current situation. Psalm 119:105 NKJV states, *"Your word is a lamp to my feet and a light to my path."* The Message Bible brings it home: *"By your words I can see where I'm going: they throw a beam of light on my dark path.*" There is nothing we have been through, are, or will be going through that is new to humanity. So, how does the Word help us? If we search it out, the Bible is full of what I like to call "pregnant voids."

A pregnant void is the space between the promise and the fulfillment. It often feels empty, lifeless, and even surreal —like it's not reality but a figment of our imagination. Yet there is life in the midst of that void, just as there is a baby in a mother's pregnant womb—hidden and unseen, an expression of explosive life held in secret for a time.

Devastation to Re-creation

Scripture itself began with a pregnant void. Genesis 1:1 says that God created the heavens and the earth. Then we jump to verse 2, where it now says, *"the earth was without form and void, and darkness was over the face of the deep."* Then comes the greatest hope anyone can possess: the fact that God was there. He had not abandoned the earth, though it had been destroyed through Lucifer being cast out of heaven to earth. (I always say you can tell where the devil is at work because there is loss, destruction, darkness, emptiness, fear, hopelessness, and lifelessness.)

In verse 2, we also see that the Spirit was hovering over the face of the waters! I want to shout this phrase out. Why? Because it's truth, and this is God's heart. He longs to create the new out of—or in the midst of—places that are destructed, leveled, and hopeless. The earth did not start out that way, it *became* that way—it became a devastated place. We are in such a place right now in many places across the world. This verse is the pregnant void between what was and what is to come—devastation to total re-creation. And the Holy Spirit is sitting in the middle of it, hovering upon the chaos!

A similar scenario occurred between the books of Malachi and Matthew in the Bible. There were 400 years of silence—four centuries of wilderness, barrenness, chaos, emptiness. There was no Word and no revelation. It was as if God was on a long lunch break and He forgot to return or was having such a good time He didn't *want* to return! I'm sure most people gave up and yielded to hopelessness and despair. They likely thought God didn't care and turned to another way, giving up their faith in Him. They turned to themselves and to other gods.

Another similar situation is found in 1 Samuel 3:1: *"Now the boy Samuel ministered to the Lord before Eli. And the word of the Lord was rare in those days: there was no widespread revelation"* (NKJV). The Message Bible restates that last phrase as this: *"This was at a time when the revelation of God was rarely heard or seen."* The King James Version says, *"there was no open vision."* That word *open* means "breakthrough." There was an absence of a revelatory word from the Lord that would release breakthrough in a dark time. It was as if the lights had gone out, and no one knew how to proceed. But why had they gone out, creating a "pregnant void"?

Eli had allowed his sons to live outside the confines the Lord had established in the Torah regarding holiness, righteousness, and priestly responsibilities. As a result, the lights —or glory—were about to go out in the temple. It was a dark time because Eli allowed compromise. His sons slept with prostitutes at the door of the temple and were subsequently called "worthless." Not only did they sin sexually, but they were ignorant of God and their priestly responsibilities. Eli was also indicted for his greed and for honoring his sons more than God. Sounds a lot like the era in which we live today, doesn't it?

Even in the dark period resulting from Eli and his sons' sin, the void was pregnant with invisible light and life. There was a plan in God's mind to restore life to Israel. God was moving in the darkness. It started in 1 Samuel 1:10 with Hannah, grieved by barrenness, crying out for a son. It says in verse 10 that *"she was in bitterness of soul, and prayed to the Lord, and wept in anguish"* (NKJV). Out of that cry birthed in her heart by God—not of hopelessness but a genuine heart yearning—came a response. She first expressed her cry to God, then to Eli. Oftentimes, we find ourselves in similar situations, grieved, wondering what's wrong with us when it's God who has put that grievous yearning in our hearts.

Samuel the prophet was the answer to Hannah's cry. God had a plan to transform what was devastated. That plan was activated in the middle of the void—the seeming darkness. Though it was unseen, God was at work. Samuel would come forth, restore righteousness and holiness, and initiate the new order, which would not only transform the imme-diate darkness but affect eternity. It was Samuel who set in order the reign of David, from whose lineage Jesus would emerge.

Hovering Until the Right Time

There are a multitude of similar examples of "pregnant voids" in Scripture.

Why do I say pregnant? Because the situation is over-shadowed by the Holy Spirit. And He is the impregnator with *life* of that which is to come. Returning to Genesis, there it was: the presence of life-giving *hope* amid devastation, emptiness, barrenness, and sin. It was the Holy Spirit. He was not one bit intimidated by that dark mess. *Hover* or *brood* is a term of impending impregnation. He hovered, brooded over, and sat on that total mass of destruction. He was carrying the seed of restoration. He was ready to impregnate and release life into a mass of nothingness. However, it was not an instantaneous response. The word *hover* implies that He sat over that area for a period of time. That also means that there was a *right time*. That period of hovering repre-sents the phase I call the pregnant void.

What was the hovering all about? It was the place or space where impregnation took place. That hovering was the space of formation from which a word would be released, like a seed impregnating the womb of creation, leading to the conception that would change everything. And how did the impregnation for re-creation take place? Through God speaking—releasing His breath of life through a "word." When God spoke, He said, "Let there be light!" That light released vision and revelation, the ability to see "the future" so that the remaining re-creation of that which needed to be reformed could once again be seen and called into existence.

In this pregnant void, God releases glory, His very essence, the substance that creates, reforms, and transforms. It is the miraculous transformational power in every word He releases. And it activates what is to be birthed. For instance, Abraham called *"those things which do not exist as though they did"* (Romans 4:17 NKJV). He was speaking into the pregnant void words that activated the new—the yet-coming birth of Isaac.

I discuss this process in detail in another book I wrote: *The Overcomer's Anointing*, Chosen Books, 2009.

Expectation Creates Faith

As I've said before, currently, we are in a critical time when God is preparing a body of people to emerge into a new dimension. We are called to be kings and priests who rule and reign with Him on the earth (Revelation 5:10). I call it God's legislative governing body who, though living in this world, is of another Kingdom, another government that trumps the one in which we physically reside. Outside of God, we cannot change anything. To bring life and restoration to the devastated areas of people, cities, and nations, we need a people who revelationally see who we are from God's viewpoint and arise, begin to say what the Father is saying, and do what the Father is doing. We need a move of God. But we are the ones who will pioneer the move of God that changes everything as we say and do what *He* is saying and doing.

We are living in a place seemingly unable to reproduce life. As a whole, we're barren—sterile, so to speak. It may not be that you and I are doing anything wrong. It's a timing issue. God is not one bit intimidated by it. He is looking for those holding on to the promise in that space between the seed and its realization: the very same place Abraham found himself in.

"Even when there was no reason for hope, Abraham kept hoping —believing that he would become the father of many nations. For God had said to him, 'That's how many descendants you will have!'" (Romans 4:18 NLT)

I believe we're currently living in a test. Will we keep hoping like Abraham did? Will we wait for God? Will we have faith for the future in the pregnant void where nothing visible is happening? Remember, faith is the substance of things hoped for, as outlined in Hebrews 11:1. Furthermore, hope, which biblically means "expectation," creates faith. Faith and hope are inextricably linked.

Expectation is a word that is alive. It's expectation that moves a child to be excited about Christmas or a special event. They are sure something good, even great, is going to happen. They're eagerly waiting with bated breath, knowing that something they can't see yet is on the way. Near the end of the movie *The Miracle on 34th Street*, the little girl sits in the backseat of the car, looking at the house she wants to live in.

It is not a reality yet. As she zeroed in on the house, she kept saying, "I believe." Faith isn't ethereal; it's a substance that is created by expectation. And this expectation is what we need in the hour we're living in—hope in chaos.

A Door of Hope

One of my many favorite verses in the Bible is Hosea 2:15. The backdrop is the story of a nation that had left its first love, personified by a woman. She had traded following God for unfaithfulness—idolatry, spiritual adultery, ungratefulness, greed, Baal worship, and immorality, to name a few! So God basically tricked her. He drew her in and enticed her into the place of trouble. He brought her into the wilderness to bring her to a place of repentance. It says in verse 14 that He *allured* her, bringing her into a wilderness where He could speak to her. She couldn't listen until she had been stripped. She had to go to the threshing floor, where all mixture would be removed. And in judgment, He remembered mercy.

Verse 15 is the zinger, though! God said that *in the middle* of her trouble, the valley of Achor (*Achor* means "trouble"), He would provide a way out. That valley of trouble would become a door of hope. In the middle of the mess, God would create a door. Remember: Hope means expectation, so that door was one of expectation. Secondly, the word *hope* also means "rope or cord." In meditating on this Scripture years ago, I imagined this rope or cord reaching through the door and pulling me through the door. In other words, it was the place of deliverance, the door of the rope, the cord where hope exploded with delivering power.

Furthermore, He would give her back her vineyards, and she would sing there. A song of joy would burst out of her after the pressing of the grapes. We can infer that through her singing, she would produce fresh wine, which speaks of joy, abundance, and favor. Wine represents a fresh outpouring of the Holy Spirit. And that fresh outpouring of wine releases celebration! This wasteland place became God's "happy hour" for Israel. Because of God's outrageous pouring out of new wine, they expressed crazy, outrageous joy. They were totally out of control with joy!

So, how does the door of hope relate to the pregnant void? The call of God to a pioneer, a way-maker, is to venture into the wilderness places—places of emptiness, chaos, and hopelessness—and bring new life into them. These spaces are uncharted territory, where there seems to be no way through and no hope to transform. It's the place between the promise and the fulfillment of the promise. The call itself allures the pioneer into the wilderness place—the dangling carrot I mentioned at the beginning of the chapter. And in that very place of destruction and uncharted territory, the way-maker will be instrumental in creating a new path that leads people out and into the new.

Abandoned to God

The wilderness we are currently in is where formation takes place, fully preparing us for what is to come. By walking off the map, obediently following a way that is foreign to us, we are delivered into the pregnant void. There, we are stripped, threshed, tried, proven, and qualified to rule with authority and power in this emerging new era.

At the end of the third chapter, I said:

> *We're now in a day where God is inviting many to [walk off the map]. He's inviting us into the more of something. It won't be comfortable, easy, or popular. It's a leap into the unknown, after all. Usually, we won't even know the ultimate results of walking off the map. Yet it's these 'abandoned to God ones' who are going to become the birthers of the next thing God is doing. They will kick-start the critical elements of the emerging new era. They are the pioneers, the forerunners. They thrive in the midst of the unknown and move from crisis to crisis, miracle to miracle because they are willing to go where man hasn't gone before.*

Now, in this space for which we now have language, it is time for pioneers to arise and take their place. They come up out of the void and respond to a call to birth the new with great expectation.

CALL FORTH THE PIONEERS!

Pioneer Story: Esohe R. Osai

> *"Righteousness and justice are the foundation of Your throne; Mercy and truth go before Your face."* (Psalm 89:14 NKJV)

"He guards the paths of justice,
And preserves the way of His saints.
Then you will understand righteousness and justice,
Equity and every good path." (Proverbs 2:8–9 NKJV)

In my early 20s, I found myself struck by an understanding of God as a God of justice. Growing up in church, we often learn about God's righteousness. But both righteousness and justice are the foundation of His throne. God's heart for justice is a constant theme throughout the Old and New Testament scriptures. Reading about this began a stirring in me to experience that aspect of God. He is a God who loves to make wrong things right.

At the time, I was finishing my undergraduate degree and preparing to begin my career as an educator. I felt God melding this stirring for justice with His calling for me to be a change agent in education. I became convinced that, in a just world, people have an equal chance at success. I started my career as a high school teacher and eventually completed a PhD at the University of Michigan. Throughout this time, I faithfully attended Apostle Barbara's church in Ann Arbor, Michigan, where I learned about being a "sent one" and pioneering works for the Kingdom. Suddenly, in dramatic fashion, God sent me to a new city: Pittsburgh, PA. I went with a calling as a type of Nehemiah, the OT hero who rebuilt the ruins. But I went alone, unsure of what God was asking me to do.

When I arrived in Pittsburgh, one specific concern that stood out to me was the seemingly limited access to post-secondary education pathways for Black youth in Pittsburgh's racially segregated neighborhoods. During my early engagements at one high school in a low-income community, youth voiced a clear awareness that their school did not have opportunities to take advanced courses. The students also knew that the high school a few miles away, mainly serving White and higher-income students, offered many advanced courses. The awareness of this disparity profoundly influenced their academic self-concept and vision for their future. Why didn't their school have equal investments in opportunities for advanced learning?

As I examined the problem, I realized that the data spoke just as clearly about the issue as the youth had spoken. The local high schools primarily serving Black youth have consistently had post-secondary education completion rates under 5%. In the same district, a school serving mainly White youth boasted that over 70 percent of their students earn a 2- or 4-year degree. Learning about these inequities launched the Justice Scholars Institute (JSI).

Working closely with the high school in my neighborhood, I pioneered a model to support educational equity in Pittsburgh by supporting opportunities for the most marginalized students in the region. The building phase was difficult, and I faced opposition. Every force of hell seemed lined up against these young people and their educational future. I felt like Nehemiah, on assignment to build a wall, with a weapon in one hand and a tool in another. But I assembled a team of co-laborers with a vision for what was possible in the lives of these young people who had been left behind.

Eventually, the work was established, and we began to see the fruit of our labor. We grew the program from one class of 13 students at one school to a program offering over a dozen courses at three schools and serving 130+ students per year. We've seen students go from homelessness to Stanford. We've watched generational cycles broken as students became "the first" in their families. We've witnessed forgotten and neglected schools become places of deep learning and engagement. God blessed me to pioneer this program, which has served as a model of what is possible. And it is His work, not mine. I was a steward of a vision that was in God's heart. After all, he is the God of justice. He loves to make wrong things right.

Esohe R. Osai
Director, *Justice Scholars Institute*
Assistant Professor, School of Education, *University of Pittsburgh*

Chapter 6

Call Forth the Pioneers

Have you ever seriously wondered about pioneers? I'd venture to guess that you've been hearing the word "pioneer" tossed around for quite some time now. I've even used it a few times in this book already! But have you ever taken time to wonder about what that word means? Who are the pioneers? What is in their heart? What are they searching for? Are they restless and uneasy, feeling like there is more? Do they feel a genuine call from God to strike out into the new, leaving life as they knew it behind?

Perhaps we need to look at history for a moment to gain insight. In the 1600s, the Pilgrims or Puritans from England were pioneers. They longed to establish something birthed in their heart in England, so they plotted to leave everything they knew to come to a new place—America. They found the system in which they lived oppressive and binding in some way. They longed for freedom, a life-giving relationship with God, and liberty to serve Him without the confines of religion. So they struck out by boat and crossed the Atlantic to find a place to build a life with God like they had envisioned in England.

Think about the phrase, "Go West, young man!" Though we still don't know who first used the phrase, we do know it was a call in the 1800s to young men to move westward, establishing new and uncharted territory. Its intent was both entrepreneurial and adventurous. That call appealed to risk-takers seeking something new and novel and, for others, discovering new places of potential financial profitability. Both younger and older men, often with their families, left the known to find something better. Some even had big ideas and visions of what they might create in previously unknown places.

The Kingdom Age

Like the pioneers in the previous paragraph, we are in a similar place right now. There is new territory to be developed. We've never been here before. Leaders continue to speak about transitioning from the Church Age to the Kingdom Age, from a pastoral local church mindset to an apostolic Kingdom mindset. But what does that mean? Well, reading the Gospels and the book of Acts, it's easy to see that the main message of John the Baptist, Jesus, and the apostles is that the Kingdom of God has come, and that message changes everything. In Matthew 4:17, Jesus said "repent, for the kingdom of God is at hand." In fact, the Kingdom of God is what I interpret to be one of the two main changes that entered the world when Jesus came. E. Stanley Jones calls them "the unshakable kingdom and the unchanging person."

A kingdom is a realm of rule headed by a king or singular ruler. All the people, land, and possessions in that realm are ultimately under the authority of the king. Are you tracking with me? The Kingdom of God is an invisible, life-giving realm of relationships, structure, and government, which I see as a benevolent dictatorship. What I mean by that is God wants to be King—Ruler in our lives *and* the earth. He desires to dictate the nature of our relationship with Him as well as others: who we are to be, what we are to do, and how we are to act. He desires absolute authority not to create puppets but to create followers who co-labor as well as co-inherit with Him, working with Him to fulfill His ultimate purpose and plan. It is both personal and corporate. However, this is a difficult concept to comprehend because we live in a democracy where everyone has a voice and a right to determine how things should be both in the government of the state/nation and in places we work and worship.

When you become a Christian, you become part of God's Kingdom or realm of rule irrespective of gender, ethnicity, social status, education, or wealth. And in this Kingdom, our responsibility is to find God's purpose and plan for us so that we can contribute to His ultimate plan. I like to think of the Kingdom Age as the second coming of the New Testament church of Acts, where people are so overtaken by God that they surrender everything to His control. It is an age where we are so filled with life, love, and faith that we go out of the walls of the church and change the world according to God's Word, will, and way.

Here is an example that may help. I have been to Singapore several times. To me, it feels like a kingdom run by a benevolent dictator. At least three main ethnicities comprise the population: Chinese, Malays, and Indians. *All* people living in Singapore surrender their ethnicity's unique differences to the ruling dictator. There is order, clarity of roles, clear rules concerning corporate and personal behavior, and firm but caring governmental oversight. Crime is almost nonexistent. There are consequences to violating the governing leader's rules of order and behavior, which maintain a morally ordered society. Historically, the last several pages of their leading newspaper, *The Straits Times*, report on the good deeds of people, like finding and returning wallets and purses to the owners. Imagine that being said of *our* nation!

The New Testament church of Acts preached the Gospel to the ends of the earth. Cities and regions were changed for the good because of the advancement of the Good News of the Kingdom. Ephesus was utterly transformed by the pioneer named Paul. Paul went where no one had gone before and radically preached the Gospel. Not only did it change the city, but it also changed the government and economy.

Can I Have It?

To transition into the Kingdom age, we must fully surrender to the King. When I became a Christian, I surrendered everything I knew at the time to surrender. I knew I had to put God at the center of my life, effectively making Him my ruler. Everything I was and possessed belonged to Him. It changed my entire life for good! Things that were destroying or undermining my integrity were eliminated as I surrendered my entire life to God. And I truly mean my *entire* life.

I'll never forget sitting in my convertible in the garage. I was getting ready to start the car and pull out, making my way toward work. Before I started the car, God asked me, "Can I have your car?"

Ouch. That was hard. I loved my car. Still, I said, "Yes, Lord." But I wasn't prepared for what was to come.

"Can I have all of your belongings in your apartment?" He asked.

By then, I realized He was making His way through every part of my life. With tears streaming down my cheeks, I said yes again. I was so overtaken that I could hardly make it to work. My eyes were stinging and swollen, weeping through the surrender. It was one of those days when the realization of the Kingdom of God confronted me in a highly invasive way. John 3:3 says that you can't see the Kingdom unless you are born-again—fully converted. So, to see *and* enter the Kingdom requires our conversion, which involves total surrender to the King. It is in that place where the Kingdom of God is both within us and at hand. We then move out and take ground with the God-given authority, miraculous power, and ability to accomplish that for which He called us. Surrender to the Kingdom—not just the local church—must be the core of the pioneer.

The Wilderness is Necessary

In Scripture, we can also gain insight into the calling and life of the pioneer. John the Baptist was certainly a pioneer. His calling was to be a voice and prepare the way for the coming Jesus. Fascinatingly enough, it was in the *wilderness* that John the Baptist was to create the way. God sure does like to use the wilderness, doesn't he? *"For this is he who was spoken of by the prophet Isaiah, saying: 'The voice of one crying in the wilderness: "Prepare the way of the Lord; Make His paths straight."'"* (Matthew 3:3 NKJV)

In this context, the word *crying* does not mean emotional distress or sorrow. It means to call out, proclaim, pronounce, shout out, and apprehend with one's voice. To declare "there is something new and world-changing on the way. Get ready!" John was a lone voice out in the middle of nowhere, clearing out a broad passageway and developing a path in unknown territory with his voice and declarations.

A wilderness is uncharted territory. It is a solitary, lonesome wasteland, a desolate, empty space lacking clarity. Confusion and chaos often abound in the wilderness. People experience dysphoria, disconnection, bewilderment, and disorientation. Temptations are rampant because no one knows where they are, and they reach for anything to soothe their sense of "nothingness"—the void, empty place.

It was in the wilderness that Jesus was tempted by Satan with three compelling temptations: 1) to turn the stones into bread, 2) to throw Himself off the pinnacle of the temple, stating the angels would protect him, thus putting God to the test, and 3) Satan promised he would give him all the kingdoms and their glory if Jesus would fall down and worship Him (Luke 4:1–12). These are enormous temptations Satan used to entice Jesus to stand in the place of His Father, God. I could say it this way: He was tempted to take matters into His own hands. And so it is with us. The temptation in the wilderness is to fail to trust God and grasp for control. I've tried that more than once, and it hasn't worked out. I will say from experience that it will only increase the negative emotional intensity of the wilderness and delay our departure date.

It's Not Too Dark for the Pioneer

Why am I saying all this? Because one of the most dangerous places seems to be the wilderness. If we don't know where we are amid chaos and confusion, it's tempting to find any way possible to escape. This place can be miserable and potentially derailing. Yet, it is the path to the promise. It's exactly where we must be.

It's in this space that the pioneer is called. The in-between place: after the promise and before the fulfillment. The longer the time delay, the greater the challenge to continue and persevere in the face of adversity. It's here that many fall off the edge. It's grueling. Emotions run rampant, our imagination spinning out of control, trying to make sense of what is happening. This is where the make-it-or-break-it time occurs. Jesus Himself had to face this reality, and He overcame it. In fact, the Word says he came out of this place with power (Luke 4:14). He had to go into the wilderness to receive fresh mantling and fresh power to accomplish his purpose.

In this new era, we must rise unafraid of the messiness, demonic assaults, and emotional attacks that occur in the wilderness. We must forge headlong into that place to create a way where there seemingly is no way. We must go into the unknown and overcome. For in overcoming, we break the power of the wilderness's voice. We will birth the voice of God with power—*dunamis*, and *exousia* power.

When I think of the courage it will take to say yes to the wilderness, I think of one friend in particular. He is called to one of the darkest cities in America. It's a waste howling wilderness. Many Christian leaders have gone into that city and fallen, their families just about destroyed or capitulated to the temptations of spiritual darkness rampant over the territory. Thus far, it's one of the darkest cities in America I've ministered in. It's one of the poorest cities in the country, as well as one of the most sexually defiled and perverted. Still, it's not too dark for God, which means it's not too dark for my friend, who is a pioneer. He's like David, who marched into the midst of the battle declaring, "Is there not a cause?" and "Who is this uncircumcised Philistine?" (1 Samuel 17:26, 29)

David was a true pioneer. He initiated a campaign of victory in a place where others only saw the potential for overwhelming defeat. In fact, most thought defeat was inevitable. Even Saul was terrified and self-absorbed and created a void in Israel through faithlessness.

Saul answered David, 'You can't go and fight this Philistine. You're too young and inexperienced—and he's been at this fighting business since before you were born.'

David said, 'I've been a shepherd, tending sheep for my father. Whenever a lion or bear came and took a lamb from the flock, I'd go after it, knock it down, and rescue the lamb. If it turned on me, I'd grab it by the throat, wring its neck, and kill it. Lion or bear, it made no difference—I killed it. And I'll do the same to this Philistine pig who is taunting the troops of God-Alive. God, who delivered me from the teeth of the lion and the claws of the bear, will deliver me from this Philistine.'

Saul said, 'Go. And God help you!'

Then Saul outfitted David as a soldier in armor. He put his bronze helmet on his head and belted his sword on him over the armor. David tried to walk but he could hardly budge.

David told Saul, 'I can't even move with all this stuff on me. I'm not used to this.' And he took it all off.

Then David took his shepherd's staff, selected five smooth stones from the brook, and put them in the pocket of his shepherd's pack, and with his sling in his hand approached Goliath.

As the Philistine paced back and forth, his shield bearer in front of him, he noticed David. He took one look down on him and sneered—a mere boy, apple-cheeked and peach-fuzzed.

The Philistine ridiculed David. 'Am I a dog that you come after me with a stick?' And he cursed him by his gods.

'Come on,' said the Philistine. 'I'll make roadkill of you for the buzzards. I'll turn you into a tasty morsel for the field mice.'

*David answered, 'You come at me with sword and spear and battle-ax. I come at you in the name of God-of-the-Angel-Armies, the God of Israel's troops, whom you curse and mock. This very day God is handing you over to me. I'm about to kill you, cut off your head, and serve up your body and the bodies of your Philistine buddies to the crows and coyotes. The whole earth will know that there's an extraordinary God in Israel. And everyone gathered here will learn that God doesn't save by means of sword or spear. The battle belongs to God—he's handing you to us on a platter!' (*1 Samuel 17:33–47 MSG)

That last statement is what a pioneer sounds like. David's booming voice shouts out from the wilderness, in this case, the most treacherous circumstance, "I'm here, and because I'm on assignment from the God of Angel Armies, things are going to change drastically. We will not be defeated. There is a new leader rising up and taking over."

In His Power

Not everyone is called to be a pioneer. It is an apostolic calling, a military-like stance—a mindset that requires an unquestionable call from God. With that call comes great faith and fearlessness, as well as God's grace to traverse every difficult situation that arises.

One key aspect of this new era is that apostolic ministry is being restored. True apostolic ministry contains an element of pioneering, as does true prophetic ministry. Look at the apostles in the book of Acts. They were trailblazing risk-takers who, when God spoke, moved out in faith and watched people and cities change when they followed God's leadership. I've already mentioned Paul, whose ministry changed an entire city, Ephesus. And it wasn't only the apostles who blazed a trail. Philip was a deacon who led the Ethiopian eunuch to a relationship with Jesus. (Acts 8:26–40) That ultimately affected an entire nation, Ethiopia. Philip met the eunuch on the road from Jerusalem, advancing the gospel to an entirely different nation.

It's time for the pioneers to come forth. Like David, they march into the enemy's territory at God's direction and devastate dark forces and evil structures ruling over cities and nations. They create springs of water in the wilderness, grow vineyards from which the new wine is produced and flows, and break through the stronghold of darkness and devastation. It is time for the *new* movement! I say to the pioneers, those called to the place of void, darkness, and devastation: This is your moment. This is what you were born for.

"But you shall receive power, (ability, efficiency, and might) when the Holy Spirit has come upon you, and you shall be my witnesses in Jerusalem, and all Judea and Samaria, into the ends, (the very bounds) of the earth." (Acts 1:8 AMPC) A new breed of

trailblazers is about to be break forth. You may be one of them. And this will not be done in your own strength but in the power, ability, efficiency, and might of God.

Pioneer Story: Jennifer LeClaire

I got a crash course in apostolic pioneering as we planted Awakening Prayer Hubs in over 100 nations, including Muslim countries. I learned true apostles don't seek titles—they bear burdens. Apostolic ministry isn't about fancy nameplates, speaking engagements, or accolades. It's about carrying the weight of the Kingdom with a deep sense of responsibility. Apostles are called to pioneer, to blaze trails where others fear to tread, and to break the hard, fallow ground for others to build upon.

Apostolic ministry isn't glamorous; it's gritty. It's sleepless nights in prayer, weeping over souls, and fighting battles in the spirit that most people don't even recognize are happening. It's birthing movements that shake regions and nations. It's the price of being misunderstood, persecuted, and even rejected—but pressing on because the mission is greater than the pain.

Apostolic ministry is about breaking ground—going where others haven't gone, dealing with spiritual resistance from which others may shrink back, and refusing to quit even when it feels like the heavens are brass.

It's about birthing movements—not just starting something but laboring in prayer, strategy, and execution until the vision comes to life. And it's about warring for territory in the spirit—pushing back demonic principalities, confronting strongholds, and standing firm on God's promises until His Kingdom comes and His will is done.

Count the Cost

This isn't for the faint of heart. It's not for those looking for platforms, applause, or followers. It's for those who are willing to lay down their lives, their plans, and their comforts for the sake of the Gospel.

Are you ready to pay the price? Are you willing to step into the fire of refinement, the weight of responsibility, and the trenches of spiritual warfare? The true mark of an apostolic pioneer is not their title—it's the scars they bear, the burdens they carry, and the lives they change for the glory of God.

Jennifer LeClaire
Awakening House of Prayer
www.awakeninghouseofprayer.com

Chapter 7

What Characterizes Pioneers

Now that we've touched a bit on the place pioneers are called to and some historical context, let's dig in a little bit more and learn about what they might look and sound like. Pioneers are a fascinating group of people who make things happen. They don't just see the future; they *create* the future. This was what characterized the church birthed on the day of Pentecost, the early church. In one moment, they were overtaken, immersed, and baptized into a new dimension that transformed them into a bold company of pioneers. They ran out of that place of encounter into the city, where Peter boldly began proclaiming the Gospel. Again, in just one moment, 3,000 people were saved and transformed into believers (Acts 2).

Pioneers are riders of the cutting edge, leaders who both create and guide the way, innovators, trailblazers, groundbreakers, initiators, fire starters. They are bold, creative, dedicated, visionary, persistent, and passionate. Pioneers are particularly needed in times of shifting, as they go before and create the new. They're change agents, original thinkers who are independent, confident, and possess an unusually positive attitude—"We can do it!" and "We won't quit!"—and release the spark that initiates change. They forge new paths and leave a mark, and it's often impossible to forget them because their impact is so significant.

As I was reviewing the edits to this book, I noticed a Facebook post by a friend of mine. This is a picture of a pioneer launching out into the new. In his words, he started life as a first-class loser. But then something dramatic happened to him. He became a Christian, a *real* Christian! Knowing and following Jesus completely turned his life upside down. After this turnaround, God gave him a vision for business, but he had no money, education, or experience. Not only did he go on to establish a successful real estate business, but he now leads and mentors many others. He's also a podcast host, author, trainer, and coach. He's a pioneer. Here is his initiating experience in pioneering, a short story that he posted on Facebook:

> *What a full-circle moment!*
>
> *Last night, I went to Fairlane Mall in Dearborn, Michigan, to pick something up—it had been years since I'd been there. Entering through the food court, I walked to this very spot, and it hit me how far I've come.*
>
> *After becoming a Christian and turning my life around, my first introduction to business was through Amway when I was*

20 years old. Back then, I was told I needed to show "The Plan" (if you know, you know) and talk to as many people as possible.

Fresh out of rehab and off the streets, I was determined to succeed because I knew God had a plan for me. I didn't have a driver's license at the time, so I'd take the SMART Bus from my home in Melvindale to Fairlane Mall. I wore a thrift store suit, carried a thrift store briefcase, and handed out Vistaprint business cards. I'd walk around the mall looking for people who seemed successful.

I was at Fairlane Mall today when I approached the exact spot where I mustered up the courage to approach a man in a suit who looked successful. Nervously, I talked to him about Amway. He rejected me completely but told me he respected my efforts.

That moment didn't stop me. I went on to learn a lot about business and found some success with Amway. Looking back last night, I realized it wasn't just about the success—it was about the determination, commitment, and will to win, no matter the circumstances. I didn't have a car or a license, but I made it work, riding the bus wherever I needed to go.

Reflecting on it all, I'm proud of myself for never giving up and never quitting. Most people see the success, but they rarely see the journey it took to get there. I realized that many wouldn't have done what I did, and most aren't willing to do whatever it takes.

Success comes with a price, and I've always been willing to pay it, no matter how hard the road has been or what I've faced.

The good news is that anyone can do it. You just have to ask *yourself: "How bad do you want it, and what price are you willing to pay?"*

ALL IN!

—Justin S. Ford, Owner of Justin Ford Real Estate Team, Plymouth, MI

As we can see in Justin's story, it's nearly impossible to dissuade pioneers to the point where they give in or give up. Roadblocks and hindrances don't discourage them; they empower them. It's like a fighter who, facing his biggest fight, is charged with adrenaline. They know that this is what they were created for. God put a spirit within them that is not easily intimidated. He created them to transform the chaotic, confusing, devastated, and desolate places. There's a voice inside of them that says, "Let me at 'em." I bet this description immediately made you think of someone just like this. Is it you?

The Driving Force of Passion

True pioneers will drive some people nuts with their passion. They'll often be told not to be so intense, not to take things so seriously, to calm down, to relax. But the truth is, pioneers *are* intense. Everything they do seems extreme. In fact, it usually *is* extreme in some manner. Remember, David ran to the giant believing he could take it out!

That passion pioneers possess creates tenacity within them. They are about serving and investing in something much bigger than themselves, sold out for whatever it is they're putting their hands to. Pioneers are willing to give their entire lives to and for "the cause."

My spiritual mother and her daughter were just like this. Myrtle D. Beall, affectionately referred to as Mom Beall, believed that God prompted her to begin a Sunday school for children in 1934. All she had was a tiny storefront building with no chairs, so she laid newspapers on the floor for the children to sit on and believed for them to show up. And sure enough, the children came. Not only did the children come, but their parents began to show up, too! They loved what their kids were being taught and wanted to learn as well. Soon, a church arose out of that simple little Sunday school. She named it Bethesda Missionary Temple, and it grew and grew some more.

Eventually, she had to transition the church from the storefront to a portable building. As the church continued to grow, they moved to a basement and, finally, to a large visible structure at the corner of Van Dyke and Nevada Street in Detroit, MI. A significant and internationally impacting revival broke out there in 1948 called the Latter Rain Revival. The church exploded to 3,500 people. Mom Beall had a burning vision in her heart that she was willing to sacrifice everything for—she gave her entire life to this church.

Let me tell you something about her that will knock your socks off. She was raised as a Catholic in the Upper Peninsula of Michigan, Hubbell, MI. She was considered a heretic when she left the Catholic Church to marry a Methodist and struggled tremendously over that decision. But she believed she had heard from God about marrying this Methodist man. Leaving everything behind, as Ruth did in the Bible, she was rejected by her family. But something was burning inside of her. Little did she know that her marriage was the positioning necessary for her to start what eventually became a mega-church when they were few and far between. Because of that marriage, she moved to Detroit, Michigan. God *wanted* her in Detroit.

She experienced a lot of backlash because she was a woman pastoring a church. In her day, women didn't lead churches. When the revival broke out, shortly thereafter, the denomination she was connected to rejected her over what they called false teaching. Even before this devastating event, I remember her recounting the turmoil she experienced as she walked out the door and down the sidewalk away from her house every day, leaving her children behind her. Tears would often stream down her eyes as she walked away from them to pastor her church. But something powerful and consuming burned within her. She couldn't lay the vision down.

Persecution surrounded her until the day she died, despite multitudes coming to know Jesus and their receiving baptism in water and the Holy Spirit with fire. Not only were people changed because of her, but the surrounding area was affected financially. Real estate prices went up, and the entire surrounding area—approximately a 2-mile radius—was radically transformed. Eventually, the church constructed about two blocks of buildings to house the work.

She was a gentle giant who, when God spoke, would act. It makes me think of the common saying, "The proof is in the pudding." Great fruit came from that simple woman who burned with a heart for God and the vision He gave her. It was simple: She moved and acted when God spoke, giving her direction. She was considered out of the box and radical, yet she remained unbeatable. She was a pioneer.

Motivation Matters

Just as we can glean from the examples of Justin and Mom Beall, we can learn about the character of a pioneer through the Bible. Paul the apostle was a true pioneer, sold out for the cause of Jesus. He kept going no matter what he faced: shipwrecks, prison, and being flogged and beaten, just for starters. Paul never backed down. In 2 Corinthians 4:1 NKJV, Paul said, *"Therefore, since we have this ministry, as we have received mercy, **we do not lose heart.**"* Then, further on in that same chapter, he laid out the life of a pioneer in verses 8–13:

> *We are hard-pressed on every side, yet not crushed; we are perplexed, but not in despair; persecuted, but not forsaken; struck down, but not destroyed— always carrying about in the body the dying of the Lord Jesus, that the life of Jesus also may be manifested in our body. For we who live are always delivered to death for Jesus' sake, that the life of Jesus also may be manifested in our mortal flesh. So then death is working in us, but life in you.*
>
> *And since we have the same spirit of faith, according to what is written, 'I believed and therefore I spoke,' we also believe and therefore speak...* (2 Corinthians 4:8–13 NKJV)

Paul knew that he had been created for such a time as this. He possessed an overarching conviction that God had chosen him to accomplish a purpose much bigger than himself. In fact, he had been apprehended by God to announce to the world that something life-changing had been released: the Gospel of the Kingdom. The message was new, as well as the assignment: to reach the Gentiles, the non-Jews. Furthermore, the *motivation* behind it all was something worth noting.

Without the right motivation, no part of God's family can ultimately be successful—that includes you and me! Jesus often spoke of the desirable, motivating force called love, and the apostle Paul wrote that it was the *love* of Christ that compelled him (2 Corinthians 5:14). His life proclaimed, "I am not my own; I have been bought with a price." Our lives should say the same.

It was love that caused Jesus to lay down his life for us— love drove Jesus to the cross. Paul knew that. And it was knowing *that love* that compelled him. Not only did he know the love of Christ, but he possessed that love for those God sent him to. Paul knew that to serve his own self was futility. It would get him nowhere fast. Paul's motivation resulted from an explosive impartation from Christ, thrusting him out in love and blazing a trail that we're still learning from today.

Courageous, Committed, and Cost-Counting

Pioneering is about firsts: developing, authoring, or origi-
nating something. Pioneers are often the ones leading the
way, being the first to accomplish something with a host of
people behind them. Because they're going ahead, pioneers
have to be radical because of the risk-taking nature of their
assignments. They are the first to break through, demon-
strating a "Breaker Mantle." (See my book *The Breaker
Anointing*.)

They're not intimidated by the possibility of failure. They
have made a decision: if they *do* fail, they will fail forward!
Nothing is too hard for them. They're ready to scale the
highest mountains, but neither are they fearful of the lowest
valleys. It's not that they particularly enjoy either, but they've
embraced the truth that to pioneer, there will be both valleys
and mountains through which they must navigate.

So, we know this calling requires the right motivation,
risk, and a radical way of living. But what else characterizes a
pioneer?

First of all, these risk-takers called pioneers are coura-
geous. They are not conformed to the world in which they
live, but they have been transformed through the power of
God, renewing their mind (Romans 12:2). They don't think
like everyone else does. The word *world* used in that passage
in Romans is *aiōn*, and it's very significant. One commentator
explained that the word in Greek suggests three different
issues—not conformed to the age or generation in which we
live, not biased by our ethnicity or race, and unbound by our

physical age. Each generation alive today holds specific mindsets that affect their perspective, such as how they view work, marriage, each other, and even how they talk. God's pioneers are to see beyond those factors if they are to change the part of the world to which they are assigned.

Second, pioneers possess extraordinary commitment. To be and do what God has called them to will cost them everything. We can even draw some parallels to the military here. Paul said in 2 Timothy 2:4 that *"no soldier gets entangled in civilian pursuits, since his aim is to please the one who enlisted him."* In other words, they don't compromise. The Message Bible says, *"A soldier on duty doesn't get caught up in making deals at the marketplace. He concentrates on carrying out orders."* In verse 2, The Message Bible says: *"When the going gets rough, take it on the chin with the rest of us, the way Jesus did."* Pioneers are so focused that they seem almost *too* committed —and to some, they are! They are so dedicated to a vision, cause, or activity that they are oblivious to alternative realities surrounding them. They are driven by an intense sense of purpose and will work day and night to see something accomplished. No other person or activity can dissuade them from their commitment; even difficulty will not deter them.

Third, they are not intimidated by the cost. They are willing to face the loss of everything. To provide some perspective, all but one of the twelve apostles were martyred. In more recent times, Martin Luther King, who faced every obstacle imaginable, took on the issue of segregation in America. It cost him his life, yet it led to significant positive change racially in America. William Wilberforce, the man responsible for abolishing slavery in England, worked four decades to see it happen. Rees Howells, who prayed England through WW2 from Wales, took a heavy hit on his physical body, which ultimately resulted in an earlier death. The New Testament Church was birthed in the midst of extreme adversity. They faced prison, beatings, crucifixion, being set on fire, and stoned. They were considered a cult, called extremists. That did not stop them.

Before WW2, both leaders and the general population in England thought Winston Churchill was too extreme, eccentric, and unacceptable. He drank too much, was crass, unconcerned with convention, and politically unpopular. Clearly, he was an outlier, not the norm. But desperate times changed leaders' minds. Churchill was selected to serve as England's prime minister and lead them through WW2.

We are at such a juncture now! Unconventional, pioneering leaders will reposition conventional leaders to the side. We are living in desperate times. Desperate times call for the radical and unconventional. When adverse situations arise, actions that may have been unacceptable in the past or considered too drastic will now become the best choice.

This new era can no longer support those seeking fame, notoriety, money, position, or status. God is calling a new breed who will rise above all the traps and give themselves without reservations, conditions, or self-promotion to answer the call. A new breed compelled by love to change the world.

Do you already know you're a pioneer, or are you sensing as you read this book that you might be? If so, this chapter is probably throwing gas on your fire. If you are not called to be a pioneer, you now know how to pray. We are in an hour where there is both the changing of an era and the changing of the guard. God is issuing a fresh call to those called to be pioneers—particularly but not exclusively the younger generation. And we need to be praying that they will hear the summons and be willing to engage with it.

Pioneer Story: Dr. MaryAlice Isleib

It was 1988, and there was increasing pressure being put on the Communist regimes of the USSR (Russia) and Eastern European countries to reform their social, political, and financial policies of oppression and control of their people, called the Iron Curtain. Of great concern was the severe religious persecution of Christians; anything at all that had to do with the gospel was strictly forbidden.

Public expression of the Christian faith and churches was against the law, and some believers were imprisoned, suffered, or even died for their faith. It was a very dark, oppressive, and fearful time for the Body of Christ in these nations. Most of the general population—millions of people —had never heard the gospel or knew of the Bible.

At the same time, believers, missionaries, and churches around the world were anticipating a great move of God in the Iron Curtain. There were intercessors behind the curtain and around the world who were contending in warfare and repentance, speaking the Word, preparing the way for the Lord to break through. Many brave believers and missionaries, including myself, risked their lives and went behind the Iron Curtain to raise up and encourage the pastors and underground churches, preach, pray, and prophesy the Word of the Lord.

It was in this setting that God called me to be part of the pioneering group that would break open the gospel in Eastern Europe, a communist block. The breakthrough came on November 9, 1989, when the Berlin Wall, a physical wall between East and West Germany, was completely crushed down, and the "door" permanently opened between East and West.

Word of Life Church and Bible School in Uppsala, Sweden, where I worked at the time, quickly mobilized every member and Bible school student to be missionaries. Our Missions Network was called Russia Inland Mission, which included Eastern Europe. The Heavens were open; we had prayed for it passionately for years. The appointed time was upon us to RUN as a historic move of God had exploded!

Thousands and thousands of people were saved, and remarkable miracles manifested. It is estimated that we directly or indirectly planted 1,000 churches all over Russia and Eastern Europe. It was a modern-day Apostolic wave that impacted a massive part of the world! I traveled all over the region, evangelizing and teaching prayer in the new churches and Bible schools.

I was 29 years old at the time and was honored to be one of many used by the Lord in this historic revival. One of my most powerful and memorable experiences was in Prague, Czechoslovakia, in March 1990. I had been invited by one of our new churches with a very young pastor and members. In their newfound freedom, they took a bold step of faith to invite the entire city, including the sick, to a meeting in one of the largest meeting halls in the city where the Communists formally held conferences.

Thousands of curious and spiritually hungry people who had never heard the gospel or seen a Bible before filled the hall quickly, with 3,500 inside and about 500 outside who listened on rigged microphones from inside, many of them ill. The front of the stage was filled with wheelchairs and stretchers and the very curious national television station.

We started the service with the host church leading in worship songs, and then I preached the Word. When I got to the altar call, the glory of the Lord filled the building and the field outside. I knew that glory from my prayer closet and other ministry times, but I had never experienced it quite like we did on that day. It was like a literal cloud consumed the room, the field outside, *and* the people. It was only the second public presentation of the gospel in that city in almost 45 years.

When I asked them to stand up and accept Jesus as their Lord, they held hands across the entire room and outside, praying with me, some weeping with new joy and hope. As I started to pray for the sick, healing manifested in the front of the stage while we laid hands on people. I watched a 5-year-old boy with a club foot condition as his feet turned outward when God's power went into him. His very anxious mother was shocked with joy as he began to try to walk normally. The Lord performed many miracles that night.

In the main hall, balcony, and outside, several were healed by the Word as they listened and responded. After the service, the church team collected some canes left in the building and wheelchairs left outside. After the service, a young woman came to the back room and told me she had a brain tumor, asking for prayer. Sometime later, she came to a meeting at the church in Sweden with her doctor's written note and clear x-ray, indicating that she was medically proven miraculously healed by the Lord that day.

The national television station was very skeptical the next day, but it did not matter. Thousands witnessed God move in front of their eyes! The Lord literally kissed the room with His power, hope, salvation, and love. We knew everything had opened—especially the Heavens—over millions of people who seemed hopeless and spiritually lost behind that Iron Curtain.

This is just one story in volumes from the historic modern-day Iron Curtain Revival, which was a release of an Apostolic movement in our generation. Russia's Inland Mission was a pioneering force in nation after nation, going far places, evangelizing, planting churches and Bible Schools, and raising leaders and ministries that to this day are very strong in region after region, building God's Kingdom.

The Lord opened a tremendous opportunity, but the cost was huge for all of us: incredibly hard work, money, time, effort, sacrifice, untold hours of prayer, rugged circum-stances, and heavy battles in the natural and spiritual realm. We gave up our lives for what God was doing that season. But, at times when the Lord of the harvest is ready and the Heavens are opened, He always has His pioneers prepared to work with Him, reaping the harvest. May He do it again, quickly, in the days that are ahead of us!

Dr. MaryAlice Isleib
www.MeetMaryAlice.com

Chapter 8

The Defining Encounter

As you may have guessed by now, pioneers are different—often *quite* different. They are unique in many ways and typically are not part of the crowd. They tend to be edgy, fidgety, constantly moving, seldom satisfied, always working, and unable to rest. They want to get on with it. It's as if they have been possessed by "something." Because of these characteristics, they can be quite difficult to live, work, or be friends with. (That does not mean they can't be great friends. Friendship with them just requires our understanding of their God identity—who they are created to be and how they function. Otherwise, we may find it too challenging.) There's something always compelling them onward. They are seldom satisfied with the "now."

It's because they see *something*. That something compels them into the next, whatever the next is—the future as they see it in their spirit, envisioning it in their head. Often, they don't even know fully what the "next" is. They see a vision, dream a dream, envision something quite different than the now. They want to engage in creating something that has not yet been realized. Furthermore, they tend to go on to the next before finishing the now.

To be a pioneer is challenging. As I've touched on already, people have mixed reactions. Some people want to be friends with them because it's exciting, never a dull moment. Others think they are crazy, hallucinating, or just plain odd. Think of John the Baptist or Elijah. (After all, John the Baptist came in the spirit of Elijah.) Elijah was intense, to say the least! One day, he was killing 400 Baal-worshipping prophets for God; the next, he was running like a scared cat from Jezebel. His emotions seemed to be all over the place. John the Baptist looked and lived weirdly. He lived in the desert and wore rough clothing made from camel hair with a leather belt. Strangely, he also ate a diet of locusts and wild honey. Imagine meeting someone like that!

I like to call pioneers "otherly." They are not your run-of-the-mill person or friend. A pioneer's life is demanding, complex, and even life-threatening. They go where no one has gone before., and they may feel what others seldom feel. Like Elijah, pioneers are often emotionally unpredictable. They are always searching, never quite satisfied. They are continually desperate. This is because something supernatural happened to them.

The followers on the road to Emmaus expressed their encounter with Jesus in a unique way: *"Were not our hearts burning within us while He was speaking to us on the road, while*

He was explaining the Scriptures to us?" (Luke 24:32 NASB 1995). Something was transpiring in the deepest part of them: a spiritual awakening and recognition of an encounter with the risen Jesus. They would never be the same.

They knew something extraordinary was happening. They did not just feel it; they "burned." It was the fire of recognition that they were dealing with something, *someone* far greater than themselves. They were ignited by the weight of Jesus's words—words with far more impact, way beyond the ordinary conversation. They were stunned by the revelation of His presence. It was not an emotion; it was a realization that Jesus Himself was in their midst, setting their hearts afire.

We All Need Something

Abraham looked for a city with foundations whose builder and maker was God (Hebrews 11:10). From the Genesis account, we know he wandered about searching for the Promised Land. At one point, he was in it and did not even know it! That search kept him going, whether he knew he was in the middle of the vision or not. He was looking for something, and he did not stop until he found it.

Moses, a "failure" by man's opinion, picked up the baton and received the rod of leadership for Israel. He led them into unknown territory, which was instrumental in the formation of Israel as an advancing nation.

Gideon thought he could create a new history for Israel

by facing off 135,000 Midianite infantrymen with just 300 soldiers.

David was captured by something when he stood up to face off with Goliath. While none of the Israeli army was willing to go up against Goliath, the teenage David took him on and defeated him.

Mary was pregnant without ever having an intimate relationship with Joseph. An angel had spoken to her—*that* was her intel that she was pregnant. Not only was she pregnant, but this baby was supernaturally conceived and just happened to be God's Son.

Every one of these Bible characters pioneered something that transformed the future. And to do so, something had to grab hold of them—some sort of compelling experience that enabled them to press forward against every adversarial circumstance and challenge. To be a true pioneer demands that you and I know that we know that we know that we know we are to do and be something extraordinary: to do something unheard of, embrace destiny, go somewhere we have never gone before, and be someone we have not quite been yet. That "something" calls us to enter a zone clearly beyond our capabilities since God never calls us to something we can do in our own strength.

The apostle Paul, afflicted by some personally distressing circumstance, had to unequivocally know he was called by God to complete his assignment. He had to remember his motivation: to be compelled by love. In 2 Corinthians 12:7–10, Paul said:

Because of the extravagance of those revelations, and so I wouldn't get a big head, I was given the gift of a handicap to keep me in constant touch with my limitations. Satan's angel did his best to get me down; what he in fact did was push me to my knees. No danger then of walking around high and mighty! At first I didn't think of it as a gift, and begged God to remove it. Three times I did that, and then he told me, My grace is enough; it's all you need. My strength comes into its own in your weakness.

Once I heard that, I was glad to let it happen. I quit focusing on the handicap and began appreciating the gift. It was a case of Christ's strength moving in on my weakness. Now I take limitations in stride, and with good cheer, these limitations that cut me down to size—abuse, accidents, opposition, bad breaks. I just let Christ take over! And so the weaker I get, the stronger I become. (2 Corinthians 12:7–10)

It was something supernatural that happened to Paul here that enabled him to continue pioneering despite his physical issues or whatever his handicap was.

The call and life of a pioneer are often so out of the box that something supernatural is required, some defining experience that is so overwhelming and convincing it totally shapes how we are to advance. Something has to so completely overwhelm us that our whole being is retooled for the future—heart, mind, and spirit. Furthermore, it is essential because a pioneer will be misunderstood by some, rejected by others, despised, criticized, called all sorts of names, and resisted by the status quo. Was this not the story of Jesus, the author and finisher of our faith? In Isaiah 53, He is called the man of sorrows. He has walked much of what we are called to walk, our great high priest who sympathizes with our weaknesses (Hebrews 4:15).

The "something" we've been talking about is an encounter. The type of encounter I'm talking about is an unexpected, unplanned, often unwanted, and undoubtedly surprising experience. It's no ordinary encounter. It's a meeting with God where, suddenly, we are yanked into a whole new reality. God has just encountered us with a mandate: a call, a mission, and a destiny. Sometimes, it's more like a sit-down where we are seemingly confronted face-to-face by God. It's not pleasant in the sense that God is asking for something beyond ourselves. Something that demands an all-or-nothing response. And we understand the implications of that confrontation. It will truly cost us everything.

Pioneers Attract Pioneers

I will never forget my ordination, being commissioned into "recognized" ministry. I was already pastoring when this happened. Previously, I had experienced several overwhelming encounters with God over my future. One particular encounter had me on my face for three days, speaking in tongues and completely overwhelmed by the Holy Spirit. I had been listening to Handel's *Messiah* at Christmas time. The words from that oratorio kept crashing over me, "Great is the Word in the company of the preachers." I was undone.

I knew it was a direct word to me. I did not leave my condo for three days, entirely caught up in God's presence and totally overwhelmed by the magnitude of the encounter. I was literally stuck on the floor before Him, weeping because I was overcome and speaking in my God-language, most of the time uncontrollably. I knew at that moment I was apprehended for something far beyond me. I felt similar to how Isaiah must have felt in Isaiah 6 when God confronted him over his destiny. I saw God. I saw the heavens. I saw the glory. I was "ruined," as Isaiah would say.

Now, let's fast-forward a few years. About seven, to be exact. I found myself on the doorstep of Christian International, led by Bishop Bill Hamon. It wasn't a place I would have chosen in the natural. I had come from a powerful church that was at the forefront of the move of God. Remember Mom Beall from the chapter before this? Well, her church, Bethesda Missionary Temple, is where I was prior to this encounter. She was a pioneer, birthing a church of thousands and hosting the 1948 Latter Rain Revival. They called her the mother of that revival.

When I arrived at Bethesda, the church had existed for many years, so it had organization: prescribed and developed biblical protocols for spiritual advancement, order, and well-developed ministries. The glory in that place was beyond words. Furthermore, I was a professor at a known secular university. I was quite the sophisticate! In reality, I had an overdose of pride, though I did not know it then.

When it came time to shoot me from the cannon, God took me from one pioneer to another—how appropriate! He took me from Mom Beall, certainly one of the most remarkable pioneers of her time, to one of the greatest fathers of the prophetic. In fact, I consider Bill Hamon to be the father of the current prophetic move. God delivered me into the mentoring hands of a pioneer. After all, pioneers attract pioneers, though, at the time, I did not know *I* was one myself.

So, there I was at Christian International in 1987 for formal ordination and commissioning. God had supernaturally led me to this place, though it was pretty strange and unpolished to my carnal senses. The ministry had just been birthed and was in the very early developmental stages. Still, from the moment I first stepped into the ministry, I knew God was saying this was home. I sensed it in my spirit.

You could liken the experience to how it may have felt walking into a brand-new homestead in the late 1800s. Imagine you are a pioneer going West to discover and steward new land and new territory. The wind is blowing, dust everywhere, and you step into a rough-hewn cabin made out of God knows what, and you hear Him say, "You're home." *That* is what it felt like walking into Christian International.

Bishop Bill Hamon laid hands on me that day and began to prophesy the call of God on my life. It was extensive, all-encompassing, compelling, and overwhelming. I immediately knew God was speaking through this man. I not only sensed it was God but was overwhelmed by it in my whole being. I was being encountered! I knew the implications of what was being released. When the session was over, I went back to my room and wept for several days. Why?

First, what God had already encountered me with personally was now being confirmed. Second, I knew the all-consuming hand of God on my life. God was calling me to give my life away to Him totally and unreservedly. I knew I was not my own; I was bought with a price. I knew God was saying, "Take up your cross and follow me." There was no uncertainty. Third, I knew it would cost me everything, including misunderstanding and rejection. That day, I entered an even higher and costlier level of pioneering that would radically mark the rest of my life.

Even If You Stumble

As I've touched on already, pioneers require attention-grabbing, significant encounters because there can be no question about their calling. The way before them is gut-wrenching and full of misunderstanding, betrayals, back-stabbing, misperceptions, and rejection. There must be an unquestionable call from God backing up what they are to give their lives to. In the secret hours of questioning and wondering, there must be an inner certainty that takes over, a firm knowing that God will see them through the seasons of trouble, seeming defeats, and failures. Otherwise, they will never make it. The degree of suffering, persecution, betrayal, and misunderstanding is too great. It bears repeating: they must know that they know that they know they are called to be a pioneer.

Pioneers often strike out on a path that nobody else they know has taken and do things nobody else has done. They stick their necks out and become obvious targets. They will make mistakes and be ridiculed or mocked, and they may even fall under the pressure. Still, the pioneers know they will be opposed by powers and principalities and the one who goes about as a roaring lion (Ephesians 6:12, 1 Peter 5:8). If they know the Word and remember their destiny encounter, though they stumble, fall, even check out for a while, ultimately, they know who backs them. They will get up and advance, even if it means they have a limp.

Remember Jacob? He had an overwhelming all-night encounter wrestling with an angel, and from then on, he had a limp. He stumbled into the future, the greatest days of his life. However, his strength was no longer his own but that of the God who called him.

For you who are pioneers, stand up and advance, even if you have to stumble into your future. God has spoken, and His word is true. He will go before you and make a way where there is no way. But He cannot act if you do not get up and embrace what He has already said to you. You must act! It's not over until it's over. And sometimes God allows the seemingly greatest failures just before the greatest successes. He wants to make sure that we know that He alone is God. Only God can bring success to the vision He's given us through the defining encounter.

Pioneer Story: Tahira Reid Smith

The Lord used my pioneering journey to draw me to him. The journey has been filled with more than two decades of *kairos* moments—before and even after I knew the Lord.

It began when I was an only child and a third grader living in Bronx, NY, with my mom and extended family. It was the year 1986. I was attending public school, and there was a poster contest where students had to draw a picture of something they wished they could have. Back then, Double Dutch jump rope was an everyday activity that girls played. I could not get enough of it, but it required having two people to turn the ropes to jump. For my poster, I drew a picture of an automated Double Dutch machine that consisted of two poles, three push buttons, and a girl jumping rope in the middle. I won first prize in that poster contest.

Years went by, and I never thought of the idea again—that is, until I was a shy sophomore studying Mechanical Engineering at Rensselaer Polytechnic Institute (RPI) in 1997. I was taking a class called Introduction to Engineering Design, and the theme was "Challenging the Limits in Sports and Recreational Activities." I enrolled in the course section with Burt Swersey because he was the instructor all the students said was the best.

In his class, students were to work individually on project ideas before being placed on a team. At first, I thought about all the typical sports like football and basketball. Then I had an "aha" moment—I remembered my third-grade idea. As I drew out sketches, my notebook exploded with ideas. Fortunately for me, Burt was a Jewish man who grew up in the Bronx and was familiar with Double Dutch. He encouraged me and spoke highly of the idea.

For the next three years, Burt became my mentor, coaching me on the design process. He was a serial inventor and entrepreneur, and he helped me get grants, win two patents, get exposure, and assemble additional design teams to work on the idea. The invention finally worked in 2000, and on February 14, 2000, I got featured in the *New York Times*. The article was called "Patents: An Inventor Makes Good on a Third-Grade Notion" and was written by Theresa Riordan. *Essence Magazine* and many others wrote about the story that year, and by August 2000, I was invited to the *Today Show*, where I was interviewed by Al Roker and Katie Couric. That year, I learned I was the first undergraduate to win a patent while still in school. In addition, the media attention I received that year was unprecedented and unusual for a student at RPI.

Imagine this young Black girl from the Bronx being the subject of such massive favor to the point of being unprecedented in the university's 176 years of existence. Something in me knew that all of this had to be God—even as an unbeliever at the time. It inspired me to start attending church with a friend who was looking for one because I knew it was God who had blessed me. Later that year, I got saved and started following Him.

There were many fits and starts on the journey with my invention and many long pauses. I went on to be the first person to enroll in a new program at the University of

Michigan called Design Science in 2006. I became a professor at Purdue University in 2011, eventually becoming the first Black woman to earn tenure in the Mechanical Engineering department in 2018, where many other interesting works were done and received media attention. Since 2023, I have been a full professor in Mechanical Engineering at Penn State University. I am one of the very few Black women (likely less than five) in the United States who have reached the rank of full professor in Mechanical Engineering in the United States and a fellow of the American Society of Mechanical Engineers.

And the invention? The story has been featured in children's books (2002), a standardized test for 4th graders in the state of New York (2017), and a special episode of Public Broadcasting Station's *NOVA Science Show* (2024). It has been displayed in the Smithsonian Museum of American History since March 2024 in an exhibit called *Change Your Game/Cambia Tu Juego*. It shows my late mentor, Burt Swersey, and me on the day the device first worked in 2000. Finally, I founded a start-up company to design, market, and sell my childhood invention to promote fitness and inspire dreamers and innovators everywhere to never give up.

Tahira Reid Smith, PhD
Arthur L. Glenn Professor of Engineering Education
Professor, Mechanical Engineering & Engineering Design
Associate Department Head, Inclusive Research &
Education, *Pennsylvania State University*

Chapter 9

Where's the Map?

"Where's the map?"

What a strange question to ask, right? The third chapter's title is "Walk Off the Map." So, if I walk off the map, doesn't that mean there is no map now? We've talked about Abraham a lot so far, and he didn't know where he was going. The funny thing is that Abraham had to "walk off the map," yet there *was* a path to get from where he started to the destination. Abraham had to step out of the known, comfortable place dripping with security and stability. Abraham could only take one step at a time. He did not know what the next step was until he took the previous one directed by God. It is a step-by-step sort of thing; you have no or little clue what the map is, and you just take the next step. It is faith fueled by hope.

The Lord said to Jeremiah in Jeremiah 29:11, *"For I know the thoughts that I think toward you, says the Lord, thoughts of peace and not of evil, to give you a future and a hope"* (NKJV).

Ironically, this verse was written in the middle of a chapter addressing Israel's captive state, providing direction on how to conduct themselves in captivity. In the very beginning of that chapter, God addressed the men, telling them to do the following things while living in captivity: build houses and live in them, plant gardens, get married, bear children, and get your children married so that the family line continues. That was the outlined pathway to their future. Following that, the Lord said that He was giving them a future and a hope, however vague *that* was. The bottom line is that even if we have some semblance of an outline, we still have to launch out toward the unknown in faith. We know, but we don't know.

Faith is inextricably linked to hope; both are intertwined with love. Remember that Hebrews 11:1 says that *"faith is the substance of things hoped for, the evidence of things not seen"* (NKJV). As we explored in a previous chapter, the simplest definition of hope we can glean from the original language of the Bible is expectation. The context in which we use the word *hope* in America is not the biblical definition; it carries the sense of a wish. "I hope you get better!" or "I hope things are well!" There's uncertainty. But biblical hope is an expectation or, as we see in Jeremiah 29, an expected *end*.

We Move, God Moves

Recently, I was looking at the life of Joseph. He fell off the map he knew when his brothers threw him into the well. A group of Ishmaelites (Midianites) came along and saved him.

However, they did not take him back to his father; instead, they transported him to Egypt. I can only imagine what he might have thought. For one thing, can anything worse happen to him? He was taken to a different land (Egypt), placed in the custody of someone he did not know, and ultimately ended up in prison. Joseph went off the grid. However, if we fast-forward, we see that ultimately, he saved his entire family and the future of Israel. While pondering this story, God gave me a framework to think about this occurrence. Here it is.

Consider these six words: promise (prophetic), people, purpose, plan, process, and prosper. God gives a **promise** to a **person** like you or me to fulfill the **purpose** for which they were born. He lays out a **plan** (although He's often very slow or sketchy concerning the details) to possess it and takes them through a **process** to ultimately **prosper** by inheriting the promise. Joseph went through this, and you and I also will as we advance.

God chose Joseph to save his family and immediately preserve Egypt, but also the future of Israel. His **purpose** was to fulfill the **promise** of family salvation if he persevered. He ended up in Egypt for that reason. This circumstance had already been prophesied to Abraham in Genesis 15:12–16. Israel was going to end up in Egypt for 400 years. Joseph was the pioneer—he initiated the **plan**. He was delivered into Egypt to start the prophetic **process**, but he did not yet know the **promise**. Still, he was the person chosen to fulfill a **purpose**—repositioning Israel in Egypt. In doing that, he had to go through another process—being rejected by his brothers, taken in slavery to Egypt, serving in Potiphar's house, thrown into prison, then delivered into Pharoah's house. Because he maintained his integrity and character throughout his prison sentence, he established favor with Pharaoh. That favor delivered him to Pharaoh, where Joseph became the prime minister of Egypt. This brought him and the nation into great **prosperity**.

Let's break this down a little further. God chooses us and calls us to something specific. Then, He gives us a prophetic promise concerning how we are to advance. However, we have to fill in the details because though it may seem clear at first, once we start on the journey, we find out it's not so clear. That's what the defining encounter in Chapter 8 is about. It's a promise God releases to His people concerning the future—a picture of our intended target to launch out toward. So, first of all, God has a promise involving our destination, as foggy and unclear as it may be. Consider Abraham. Scripture seems to clearly say that he didn't know where he was going. That's the conundrum of a pioneer.

By an act of faith, Abraham said yes to God's call to travel to an unknown place that would become his home. When he left he had no idea where he was going. By an act of faith, he lived in the country promised him, lived as a stranger camping in tents. Isaac and Jacob did the same, living under the same promise. Abraham did it by keeping his eye on an unseen city with real, eternal foundations—the City designed and built by God. (Hebrews 11:8–10 MSG)

The crazy thing about pioneering is there truly is not a map. We have a promise, our hope or expectation, in which we plant our faith. Faith is beginning to move forward, taking the first or next step even if you believe or feel you don't know what you're doing. When the Israelites crossed the Jordan (which God told them to do), the waters did not part until they began stepping into the river. They did not wait for the miracle before they moved. They moved, and then God moved, and then the miracle happened. Too many people wait for the way to be opened before they take a step and wonder why nothing ever happens.

This whole concept of not having a map isn't alien to me. God set me up to do something absolutely beyond my desire and ability. He gave me an impossible assignment. Needless to say, I felt overwhelmed, filled with trepidation, and even questioned why God asked this of me at my most vulnerable and weakest point. In my mind, there was no way that I could do what He asked me to do. Yet, at that very breaking point, I found the courage and faith to move forward and take the next step because I knew God asked it of me. It was not about me; it was about God.

Over time, I kept coming to a point where my back was up against a wall, even when I took the next step. Each subsequent step started with the necessity for another miracle. It required fresh faith. And my faith was connected to the initial prophetic promise from God.

Today, I am continually progressing—one step at a time.

Is There a Plan?

So, what is the plan we talked about at the beginning of this chapter? It's the footpath that only unfolds step by step. When I first moved out into this new era of ministry, people kept asking me what the plan was. They even asked me to do something—or anything, for that matter—that made it look like I was going somewhere. But I could not answer those questions. I'm sure it was very frustrating for them. It was also extremely frustrating to me! By nature, I'm an incredibly focused and deliberate person. But when I received the prophetic promise over my life, God made it very clear to me that I was not to take a step without His direction. I was not to rebuild what was or what had been.

Like many of us, I love certainty, clarity, stability, and familiarity. At that time, I didn't seem to have any of that and felt like a fish out of water. Yet something profound was happening. I had to trust the plan, even though it didn't unfold as fast as I would have hoped. To be successful, pioneers must both know and learn to be obedient to the direction God has given them. That was me; that was the plan.

God said to Mary, the mother of Jesus, that *"with God nothing is ever impossible and no word from God shall be without power or impossible of fulfillment"* (Luke 1:37 AMPC). Pioneers must know this deep in their spirit if they are to apprehend the promise and endure the process.

But what is the *process* anyway? It's a series of actions or steps taken in order to achieve a particular end. "To be processed" is to have some sort of treatment to preserve something, make it safe, or change its taste or appearance. You and I both go through a process *and* become processed. We have walked out God's orders that result in us being preserved, secured, and looking more like Him. The process transforms us for the good. Each step we take in faith aligns us more closely with God— with His Word, will, and way—and transforms us into the image of Christ. Pioneering is always a bilateral achievement: a goal is reached, *and* we are changed in the process.

In walking out the process, we can be trapped by the prevailing culture of success. Success is not necessarily in the number of people or amount of money procured. The measure of success is in the fulfillment of the prophetic promise. Have we apprehended what God has asked us to apprehend? Though our assignment is to grab hold of the promise, God is looking to see if we have been obedient to the vision, bringing His purpose into being on earth.

I spoke about the process above, which is required to fulfill the purpose of realizing the vision or reaching the goal. One aspect of that process is the development of the character of the pioneer. Pioneers do not begin implementing their mission/vision with perfect character qualities. The main issue is getting started. However, the character quality development is part of the process for the pioneer. It's in the process that character is perfected and matured. So, what are some of the character qualities God is looking to perfect through the process?

The Qualities of a Pioneer

Earlier, I wrote about God asking me to do something beyond my capabilities. I soon realized it had nothing to do with my abilities; it had to do with what God had asked of me. During that time, He drove home four qualities He was looking for: profound humility, surrender, brokenness, and repentance. These four things mark pioneers possessed and processed by God.

The apostle Paul mirrored these four qualities. In Philippians 3:4–6, he outlines his profound personal experiences and the reasons for his fame. His accomplishments before his conversion were beyond impressive, but in verses 7–8, he considered them all nothing.

> *The very credentials these people are waving around as something special, I'm tearing up and throwing out with the trash—along with everything else I used to take credit for. And why? Because of Christ. Yes, all the things I once thought were so important are gone from my life. Compared to the high privilege of knowing Christ Jesus as my Master, firsthand, everything I once thought I had going for me is insignificant—dog dung. I've dumped it all in the trash so that I could embrace Christ and be embraced by him. I didn't want some petty, inferior brand of righteousness that comes from keeping a list of rules when I could get the robust kind that comes from trusting Christ—God's righteousness.* (Philippians 3:7–8 MSG)

In Galatians, Paul stated a similar heart posture in

another way. He pioneered the Gospel to many regions and nations, experienced profound encounters, and appeared before kings and spiritual leaders. Yet none of that phased him. In his fulfillment of the prophetic promise and vision, it was *God* he wanted to make famous.

> *Indeed, I have been crucified with Christ. My ego is no longer central. It is no longer important that I appear righteous before you or have your good opinion, and I am no longer driven to impress God. Christ lives in me. The life you see me living is not "mine," but it is lived by faith in the Son of God, who loved me and gave himself for me. I am not going to go back on that.*
> (Galatians 2:20 MSG)

Paul exemplified both profound humility and surrender to God's will for him. He also demonstrated brokenness. Many people hate the word *broken* because they don't understand it. To be broken in this context does not mean you have fallen apart in pieces like Humpty Dumpty. When a horse is *broken*, he is no longer wild, unruly, rebellious, or stubborn. He has learned to be obedient to his master. A broken horse responds to the gentle pull of the reins. The trainer does not have to jerk them this way and that; all it takes is a little tug. He knows the leading and voice of his trainer and responds accordingly. His will has been handed over to the will of his master.

Pioneers yield their will to the will of their master, Jesus. In our case, God holds the reins in His hands. The ultimate goal is a total takeover by God—becoming possessed by the will of the trainer. But it doesn't happen overnight! It is, yet again, a process. However, it's worth it. Pioneers who have willingly handed over their all to God are the most powerful and successful.

Lastly, pioneers are repentant. That's another misunderstood word. Repentance is often used solely in the context of repenting from sin. It is a profound change of mind and heart that involves turning away from sin, but it is much more than that. It means to change one's mind and heart, which results in a behavior change. It might be interpreted this way: "I changed my mind because I had a revelation that affects my heart posture and transforms my behavior. Now, I think about and perceive things in a totally different way." John the Baptist linked it with behavior when he said, *"Bear fruit in keeping with repentance"* (Matthew 3:8). In other words, "Don't just tell me you have changed your mind and heart about something; let me see the difference in your life— your external behavior—as a result of that change."

Prosper

The ultimate end to every promise is inheritance. Inheritance is the "prize" of persevering to the end. In Revelation 2 and 3, the apostle John said (in my words), "If we overcome, we will inherit something." Each of the seven churches received a specific promise about what they would inherit IF they overcame. So it is with us. If we persevere through every test, every problem, every challenge, there is a prize at the end. That prize is prospering in some way—there is something that we apprehend tangibly. Ultimately, Abraham obtained the son of God's promise. Joseph prospered in his positioning in Egypt (from the pit to the palace) and in the restoration of his family. Jacob also prospered financially and familially; the most significant prospering was birthing the nation of Israel through his 12 sons representing the 12 tribes of Israel. Mom Beall was to raise up an armory, the prosperity actualized through both the realization of a mega church and territorial transformation. Charles (Daddy) Seymour birthed a revival that transformed the church *and* a nation. William Wilberforce prospered by apprehending his God-birthed mandate to stop the selling of slaves on the English slave blocks. Martin Luther King prospered through the changing of race relations in America. All of this takes an intangible substance called faith!

Extravagant Faith

As we near the end of this book, I want to emphasize the importance of something we've been touching on throughout these chapters: a true pioneer receives a prophetic promise or vision—one that always exceeds their natural ability to accomplish. It demands audacious faith and complete surrender to God, allowing His vision to unfold through them. The journey toward aligning with God and pursuing the fulfillment of His promise is filled with uncertainty, ambiguity, risk, and an ever-present need for unwavering faith. Questions and doubts will arise, but this very process compels pioneers, to adopt a posture of profound humility and repentance. These attributes are often forged through painful and seemingly impossible experiences, producing a brokenness that reflects total dependence on God. As we've seen so many times already, Abraham serves as a powerful example—a pioneer who stepped out in faith toward a promise he could not fully comprehend, journeying into the unknown simply because God called him. It is no wonder he is known as the father of faith.

So the promise is received by faith. It is given as a free gift. And we are all certain to receive it, whether or not we live according to the law of Moses, if we have faith like Abraham's. For Abraham is the father of all who believe. That is what the Scriptures mean when God told him, "I have made you the father of many nations." This happened because Abraham believed in the God who brings the dead back to life and who creates new things out of nothing. Even when there was no reason for hope, Abraham kept hoping—believing that he would become the father of many nations. For God had said to him, "That's how many descendants you will have!" And Abraham's faith did not weaken, even though, at about 100 years of age, he figured his body was as good as dead—and so was Sarah's womb. Abraham never wavered in believing God's promise. In fact, his faith grew stronger, and in this he brought glory to God. He was fully convinced that God is able to do whatever he promises. And because of Abraham's faith, God counted him as righteous. And when God counted him as righteous, it wasn't just for Abraham's benefit. It was recorded for our benefit, too, assuring us that God

will also count us as righteous if we believe in him, the one who
raised Jesus our Lord from the dead. (Romans 4:16–24 NLT)

This is a call to extravagant faith—faith that calls those
things that are not as though they are. It's the scary step of
stepping out of the boat onto the water, not knowing if we'll
be able to walk. It's beyond any assignment you've said yes to
before. But it's the faith that births the miraculous. Are you
up to obeying the call?

Pioneer Story: Elizabeth Doyle

Just before my 65th birthday, I found myself reflecting on
nearly five decades of ministry. My Irish husband and I had
spent 25 incredible years planting churches in England,
raising two amazing children, and shepherding hundreds
who would go on to spread the Gospel worldwide. Then, in
1996, God expanded my calling, taking me to 60 nations
across six continents to empower women to share the Good
News in their homes and communities.

One day, as I watched a state inauguration, my heart
broke. Certain women in leadership displayed behavior and
values that clashed deeply with my own—dishonoring their
positions with vulgarity and disrespect. Turning off the TV, I
knelt at my prayer chair and cried out, "Lord, what are You
going to do about this?"

His reply pierced my spirit: *"It's time for Christian women*
in Michigan to rise up and have a voice."

The very next Sunday, while visiting a church, I stood to

give a greeting, and the Spirit of God overwhelmed me. A prophetic word poured from my mouth: It was time to obey God's call and help Christian women find their voice. That moment sparked a movement I could not yet imagine.

As I sought the Lord's guidance, His plan unfolded step by step. I met with my state representative, who agreed to host a tea party at Michigan's State Capitol to honor Christian women who are making an impact. With faith, I estimated a $2,000 budget, but God had bigger plans. He prompted me to double it, and the very next day, a stranger handed me a $2,000 check, saying, "The Lord told me to give this to you."

In September 2019, we hosted the first She Leads Michigan Afternoon Tea Party, celebrating 80 women leaders from education, business, ministry, and government. The room was electric with encouragement as women realized they were not alone in their callings. From that seed, She Leads Michigan blossomed into a powerful network with weekly prayer calls, annual gatherings, and a focus on faith-based solutions to modern challenges.

By 2020, God expanded the vision. We launched She Leads America in Washington, D.C., hosting Congressional breakfasts, a gala at the Museum of the Bible, and a historic gathering at the Lincoln Memorial. Dr. Alveda King joined us, delivering her uncle's iconic *I Have a Dream* speech as we celebrated women making a difference.

Today, She Leads has grown into a global movement, with chapters in 12 states, including California, where we held events at the Nixon Library. In 2024, She Leads UK launched with a historic gathering at Windsor Castle, uniting women to address issues like ethnic harmony and the dignity of women. From there, She Leads Pakistan and She Leads Native America were born, furthering our mission to equip women as solutionaries across diverse backgrounds.

What began during a hostile political climate and global pandemic—with no budget, name recognition, or influential contacts—has become a multi-ethnic, non-partisan movement crossing barriers and fostering fellowship.

As Psalm 23:5 declares:*"You prepare a table before me in the presence of my enemies; you anoint my head with oil; my cup overflows."*

God's faithfulness is undeniable, and the best is yet to come.

Elizabeth Doyle
Founder, *She Leads America*
www.sheleadsamerica.com

Chapter 10

Force, Momentum, Movement

As I have reiterated before, we are in a new era that demands the birthing and assigning of pioneers who can carve the path into the new. Biblically, this is referred to several times. It's as if God is saying, "I will lead you in a way you don't know. You're blind to the path, so I'm going to help you."

> But I'll take the hand of those who don't know the way, who can't see where they're going. I'll be a personal guide to them, directing them through unknown country. I'll be right there to show them what roads to take, make sure they don't fall into the ditch. These are the things I'll be doing for them— sticking with them, not leaving them for a minute. (Isaiah 42:16 MSG)

This is a powerful, encouraging passage to pioneers, impregnating them with confidence when they receive a call, a mandate, but have no idea how to accomplish it. Pioneers are called to travel a formidable unknown path and carry out an impossible plan. That plan usually results in some kind of significant transformation and/or reformation. Jesus is the ultimate example. He is the way maker—the one who carved a new path for all of creation, a path that would enable us to transform not only individuals but entire cities, states, and nations.

In Mark 16, Jesus addressed individuals with the call to make disciples of other individuals. However, the call in Matthew 28 is monumental. In Matthew 28:19, He commanded us to go into *all the world* and make disciples of *all nations*. That's one tall order. It demands a movement for its fulfillment. Some good news for us here is that through Jesus' life, death, and resurrection, He removed every obstacle to our success by modeling the way for us. He took back the authority and power Adam forfeited and gave it back to us. He made a way through both the laying down of His own life and His formation of a critical mass of "world changers"—a *force*. However, there is a progression that must take place for this to occur.

Creating a Force

In Hebrews 12:2 NIV, Jesus was called "the pioneer and perfecter of our faith." In other words, He is the prime example for us. If He simply continued standing and remained alone, nothing would have happened; nothing would have come out of His sacrifice. However, His mandate was to lay the foundation for the greatest grassroots movement the World has ever seen, even to this very day. Jesus knew He had to pioneer something to fulfill the reason for which He came—He had to create a **force**. And He accomplished this through 11 of the 12 disciples who gathered around Him.

Following the example of Jesus, we see that pioneers have to gather a force to build with them to continue the journey. This is critical to our success as the force lays out the scaffolding. First, a force; that force creates a spark. The spark ignites momentum, which builds and finally erupts into a movement.

Pioneers spark movements driven by a contagious passion to transform and reform what deeply inspires them. In the beginning stages, they seek out three to four like-minded individuals to form a core group united in heart, mind, and spirit. This dynamic is reflected in 1 Chronicles 12, where David's mighty men—those who shared his vision—became an unstoppable force committed to rallying Israel against its enemies. Just as David needed a few trusted companions to initiate action and lead the charge, every movement begins with a small group of individuals bound together by a shared purpose determined to bring about change. It is this initial force—four to five people united in vision—that sets the stage for transformation. First, a pioneer; next, a force.

Finding those who will become the force is not easy. It's a

process where several, even many, are drawn to a leader. Pioneers are usually magnets to others. However, of all those drawn to a leader, most are unwilling to pay the price for being part of the force. First, they must fully believe in and commit to the leader's vision. Then, they must pay the price, the sacrifice of becoming part of this powerful core group. To be part of a pioneering force requires team members who are fully committed. It will cost them pieces of their life like time, money, relationships, sleep, meals, and certainly comfort. Just as the leader must be all in, so must those who become the core "force" gathered around the pioneer.

The pioneering leader must also hear from God as to who is to be one of this group *and* evaluate their character, qualifications, and level of commitment. Some primary qualifications are being faithful, available, submitted, and teachable. They must also know the Word, be people of prayer, and be radical worshippers of God. They must not fear controversy or the unknown.

This is often a painful process for the leader and those being vetted. It often comes with tension, disagreements, and agonizing relational conflicts, which can ultimately result in being qualified or disqualified. The pioneer may endure rejection, betrayal, character assassination, under-mining, misunderstanding, and other difficult circum-stances. Remember, Jesus Himself had disciples who competed with each other for front and center. He also had Judas, who betrayed Him! And these are just a couple of issues Jesus experienced. But it is worth it.

Momentum to Build

Once this powerful force gels, formed by a core group of like-minded individuals gathered around a pioneering leader, it carries such compelling energy that it naturally draws others to its cause. As more like-minded (in mind, heart, and spirit) people join, **momentum** begins to build, and with each addition, the energy intensifies. Eventually, this momentum reaches a tipping point, transforming the group into a full-fledged **movement**. Once established, the movement gains the power and authority to effect the change it was created to bring about.

Let's again consider Jesus. He came into the world as an individual with a mandate—a purpose to accomplish. We see his story begin as a baby, then as a 12-year-old, then as a carpenter until finally, at age 30, people start to know Him as Jesus the Christ, the Anointed One, the Pioneer, the Author and Finisher of our faith. By the time we get to this part of the story, He's been processed and is now ready to initiate what will become the greatest movement of all time. He draws men to Himself with the words, "Come and follow Me."

At this point, a critical mass, a force forms. That force gains momentum as people are impacted in new and transforming ways, and the multitudes begin to gather. The sick are healed, demoniacs are delivered, and people speak supernaturally in languages they've not learned at home nor ever gone to school to learn. Blind people suddenly see, lame people walk, and mentally deranged people are suddenly lucid. It's incredible! Whatever *this* is, people begin to come in droves because this pioneer carries something supernatural that draws them in. It transforms them.

Jesus Himself identified the "draw factor" in Luke 4:16–20 (MSG):

> *He came to Nazareth where he had been raised. As he always did on the Sabbath, he went to the meeting place. When he stood up to read, he was handed the scroll of the prophet Isaiah. Unrolling the scroll, he found the place where it was written,*
>
> *God's Spirit is on me; he's chosen me to preach the Message of good news to the poor, sent me to announce pardon to prisoners and recovery of sight to the blind, to set the burdened and battered free, to announce, 'This is God's time to shine!'*
>
> *He rolled up the scroll, handed it back to the assistant, and sat down. Every eye in the place was on him, intent. Then he started in, 'You've just heard Scripture make history. It came true just now in this place.'*

The draw factor was the Spirit! Jesus came in the power and authority of His Father, empowered by the Spirit of God. He both transformed and reformed those with whom He came in contact.

A Movement That Can't Be Stopped

Through the ministry of Jesus, we see that first, a **force** gathered, creating **momentum**. But it didn't stop there. That momentum was transformed into a worldwide **movement** on the Day of Pentecost.

The movement begins in Acts 2:1–11 (MSG)

When the Feast of Pentecost came, they were all together in one place. Without warning there was a sound like a strong wind, gale force—no one could tell where it came from. It filled the whole building. Then, like a wildfire, the Holy Spirit spread through their ranks, and they started speaking in a number of different languages as the Spirit prompted them.

There were many Jews staying in Jerusalem just then, devout pilgrims from all over the world. When they heard the sound, they came on the run. Then when they heard, one after another, their own mother tongues being spoken, they were blown away. They couldn't for the life of them figure out what was going on, and kept saying, 'Aren't these all Galileans? How come we're hearing them talk in our various mother tongues?

Parthians, Medes, and Elamites;
Visitors from Mesopotamia, Judea, and Cappadocia,
Pontus and Asia, Phrygia and Pamphylia,
Egypt and the parts of Libya belonging to Cyrene;
Immigrants from Rome, both Jews and proselytes;
Even Cretans and Arabs!
'They're speaking our languages, describing God's mighty works!'

This freshly launched event through an amazing Holy Spirit encounter quickly gained momentum. Why? Because something supernatural had overtaken the 120 people. They ran out into the city square where it was obvious to those who had gathered from all over the world that something "beyond" had just overtaken this group. Peter suddenly emerged as the leader of this group and began to preach powerfully to these foreigners. Three thousand of those present were riveted, convicted by Peter's message, and immediately became followers. Momentum had now been birthed, and the movement was springing forth.

A more modern-day example of this is the Civil Rights Movement initiated by Dr. Martin Luther King in 1954. He agonized over his fellow African Americans' plight created by segregation. Yes, changes had been made to their status in the United States, but much was still to be done. King rose up with a fire burning in his heart to change the oppression they experienced. Those with a similar burden joined him, and a core group that was a force for change formed. A brilliant orator, King began to herald the message, the call, the challenge, and many began to hear the "sound" that resonated in their heart and spirits and gathered around to join the force. Momentum erupted, and within a short period of time, a movement began. Ultimately, Dr. King, along with his core group and the multitudes that had gathered with them, changed the course of Black people in America. Segregation was dismantled because one man had a dream, formed a force, and gained momentum. But the price they had to pay was great. Black leaders faced lynchings, torture, being lit on fire, beatings, humiliation, and every imaginable degrading action. It didn't stop them. They persevered through every obstacle to win the prize—the undoing of segregation.

Will You Accept the Call?

Both of these examples are *societal* transformations. And we can see those types of transformations in our day if we would heed the call of God. Today, many pioneers need to become either aware or responsive to the fire that burns within them. For some, it may be to transform our extended family or become rescuers of human trafficking. For others, it may be to develop nation-changing strategies, transform the plight of the poor, or develop innovations that save lives. Whatever it is, we have to acknowledge it and act.

As I've said so many times already, we are in a new era. This calls for a *new breed* of pioneers. We have at least a couple of generations alive now who have never experienced a revival—a true move of God. Over 50% of Americans, not just outside but inside the church, are captured by pornography. I could go on and on about the challenges presenting themselves and the way they show us the need for a new path. Arenas such as government, education, social systems, and economic realities are desperately calling for the pioneers. Will you answer the call?

Look—a new era begins! A king will reign with righteousness, and his princes according to justice! A man will be a hiding place from the stormy wind and a secret shelter from the tempest. Life will flow from each one, like streams of water in the desert, like

the refreshing shade of a massive rock in a weary, thirsty land.
Then at last, eyes that are ready to see will finally be opened!
Ears that are ready to hear will finally be opened! The hearts of
those who were once hasty to form opinions will finally under-
stand and know. And those with stammering tongues will speak
dazzling truths! The fool will no longer be called Your Honor, nor
the scoundrel highly respected, for the fool is recognized by his
foolish words. Their minds plot treachery, they excel in ungodli-
ness, and they say misleading things about Yahweh. They refuse
to feed the hungry or give drink to the thirsty. The deceiver's
schemes and plans are evil. He schemes of cheating the poor,
even when their plea is just. But a person of honor has honorable
plans, and his integrity gives him security. (Isaiah 32:1–8 TPT)

That scripture should light a FIRE in you! This is the era
we are moving into. So, I now ask, what is burning inside of
you? What is beckoning you to awaken and come forth as a
pioneer? I implore you to step into the calling of a pioneer
leading us into the new; become a pathfinder, a way maker, a
voice calling in the wilderness and uncharted territory:
"Repent, for the Kingdom of God is at hand." Together, we
will see a new path emerge and a world transformed.

This is the *kairos* (opportune) moment, the right time for
the birthing of a whole new generation of pioneers. God is
calling some of you—actually, I believe there are many—to
come out of the comfortable, mundane life of certainty to be
overtaken by a whole new mantle of anointing: the Pioneer
Anointing. He is challenging you, daring you to go where no
man has gone before. Awaken, arise, and stand to your feet!

Release the good news that God has entrusted to you wherever you are called.

Awaken the Generations!

Ignite Change Agents!

Blaze New Paths!

Chapter 11

Bonus Chapter:
Pioneering Together by Benjamin Deitrick

The westward expansion was one of the most incredible phenomena in the development of the US over the last several hundred years. Most define this period as the time when America began expanding its interests and territory west of the Mississippi River, from the East Coast to the Pacific Ocean. Most people agree that it began with the Louisiana Purchase and continued through about the middle of the 19th century.

One of the things that marked this season was a concept that many refer to as "manifest destiny." This concept could be summated in the belief that the expansion west was more than just a "good idea." It was stated by many at the time that the US was "destined" to expand. It was not "meant" to stay in the defined areas that they had already occupied; rather, expansion was a divine idea and assignment.

In many ways, as we look at where we are at in "the church," especially in this season, the Kingdom of God is in a season of incredible expansion. There are so many opportunities on the horizon and much to be explored and built. But it won't happen if, as each generation, we "go our own way." We need one another. It's time to build and expand together as a company of pioneers.

The Bible states in Malachi 4:6 that before the coming of the "great and terrible" day of the Lord, God Himself would turn the hearts of the fathers to the children and those of the children back to the fathers. This scripture must mean that in many ways, in the season prophetically spoken of and foretold by Malachi, there would be a need for a great "turning back" to one another. However, somewhere along the way, the generations have become estranged and need reconnection, recalibration, and re-engagement with one another for the effective manifestation of the will and heart of God for our time.

When we evaluate the world we live in and the church as we perceive it, there are some massive gaps between the generations. Some of this is typical and present in every age that we have in recorded human history, but right now, there is an element of pain, virulence, and angst that goes beyond the normal or "natural" progression of time and "changing of the guard" between the generations. These rifts must be breached if we are to fulfill our destiny and expand the Kingdom like the US expanded the nation. There is a manifest destiny for us to fulfill... and it won't happen without one another.

Let's delve into a hypothetical story, draw parallels and

truths from the example of the westward expansion I used, and take a little imaginative journey together.

Imagine a scenario in your mind, if you will. The year is 1805, and a family has decided to move from Jamestown, NY, to pursue a life in the West. "Westward, ho!" is the cry and call, and the family sets out on this journey. Three generations have decided to go: a set of grandparents, parents, and children. This family bravely embarks on their adventure, and as they go, they endure freezing temperatures, wild animals, swollen creeks and rivers, and a seemingly endless journey through miles and miles of rugged terrain and wilderness, seeking a destination they have never seen before. There are no maps for much of their journey. They are pioneers in every sense of the word.

As the journey goes on, it becomes clear that they all present challenges and benefits to the overall success of their journey. The older generation's largest challenge is the physicality of the journey. It's hard on their bodies to bob up and down in the wagon as mile after mile stretches on before them. The temperature and barometric changes cause their joints to ache as the trip starts to tell on them. But they offer something as valuable as gold: their knowledge. You see, this particular generation journeyed by sea from Europe to the "new world" many years ago, long before their children who are on this journey with them were alive. They know a thing or two about pioneering and the psychological fortitude it takes to stay focused on your destination when it feels like you will never get there.

They know how to follow the stars and chart a course,

moving steadfastly in the direction that they want to go—even without "modern" instruments and maps. They know how to preserve the food so it doesn't spoil, ration it, prepare it on the "go" and more. They encourage their children, the next generation down, to persevere and never give up. Their previous voyage has prepared them to partake in this "manifest destiny" they are now engaged in.

The next generation's greatest weakness is a lack of knowledge in certain areas, which is the very thing that the generation above them possesses. They have never been on a journey like this. When their parents landed in the new world and were born, they saw the struggle for survival and establishing a life, building a livelihood, fitting into society, and more. But most of what they have known is maintaining what was already pioneered, not pioneering it themselves. Now, they find that they are in the pioneering seat and are bearing the main weight of responsible action to fulfill the goal and settle in a new place westward.

Their greatest strength is just that—their strength. The man's hands hold the horse's reins as they traverse the long westward road. He fixes the buggy as repairs are inevitably needed, re-shoes the horses, cuts the wood, makes the fire ready, fights off the wild animals, and hunts and shoots game for their food and provision. The woman's clever hands prepare the meals, mend the clothes, administer medicinal cures derived from the herbs in nature, comfort the children, and read to and teach them as they go along. Together, this couple provides **the hands and feet** needed to journey forward while the generation above them fulfills the role of **the mind.**

The children are the last generation. Their contribution is very different because it's not in the present but in the future. Their greatest weakness is the combination of the older and middle generations. They are lacking in both knowledge and strength. They have neither and, as such, must be taught, protected, comforted, nurtured, and carried into this potential future the family is seeking. But *their* greatest strength lies in the gift of their very person—the fact that they represent future generations. They have a seed of potential in them. In fact, without them, in some ways, the journey is pointless for the older generations; why not just stay comfortably where they were and live out the rest of their days?

The children might represent **the heart** in many ways. For the middle generation, the children are the impetus and motivation for making the journey and finding a better life. This seed for the future encapsulates hope and meaning and makes the struggle of the journey worth it in every sense of the phrase. In order to go together, they must work together. To arrive as one whole family unit, they must learn to derive the strength and motivation of each generation and move in unity to prosper in the present and the future.

There are many truths we can pull out of this hypothetical example for the current state of the church. First, it is essential to note that there are three generations involved. That is significant to us because as the current generation of leaders begins to pioneer into new territory, working with the older generation who have come before and gleaning from their wisdom, what we build in this season impacts and affects those coming behind us all! What are they seeing? Are they seeing clear, functional unity or a lot of drama, infighting, and arguments?

What we pioneer together now is what speaks into and sets the order for the future of those who come after us. Imagine if the parents and grandparents in the example above couldn't agree or work together. It would have been a disaster. Let's look at this and a few more issues here.

Experimental Truth vs. Experiential Truth

One of the issues related to pioneering together is the matter of experiential and experimental truth. Experiential truth is, by and large, what the older generations have. I'm not saying the younger generations don't have any, but let's be realistic here; you can only truly know and understand what you have actually lived. By way of the years lived and experiences, the older generation cannot help but possess massive amounts of experiential knowledge. Just like the grandparents mentioned in the story above possessed the incredible experience of making a sea journey from Europe to the US, the older generation in our day and age has what we need. They possess the knowledge of several moves of God and decades of leadership, struggles, failures, successes, hardships, and joys.

However, this knowledge sometimes makes it hard to make way for the next generation, which, by and large, relies on **experimental knowledge**. They haven't lived, endured, struggled, hoped, or dreamed through what the older generation has, but they are excited to see what's possible. This is a tremendous strength. In fact, no great innovation has ever been achieved without taking the risk of experimenting. The younger generation in the story above experiments with taking the risk of the westward journey! They don't know what they will find, but for the joy of the potential blessings of a different life and future, they endure the risks of the experiment.

The older generation on that journey might have had the temptation to say to them, "That won't work. We never did it that way before." And this may be wisdom at times. There are certain principles and skills they learned on their journey that are more than applicable in the new journey of pioneering westward. These insights are valuable; however, they are not always right. In science, sometimes saying, "This is how we've always done it" causes roadblocks to innovation. The "way it's always been done before" didn't achieve the desired outcome for innovation. The experiment *is* needed, and the risk *must* be taken!

To truly walk off the map, we must abandon how we have always done it and launch out into unknown territory. This might be hard for the older generation, fearing the pain of failure that the next generation might endure if they abandon the old ways to experiment and innovate for the current solution that is needed. But this risk is the very thing that drives innovation forward, bringing cures and solutions and breakthroughs in technology and more to spring forth.

So, you might ask, "What is the right way to do it?"

"Both" is the answer. Both ways and opinions are needed to move forward. We need the foundation of experience—of what is known for sure—to have the context to launch into the unknown. Together, they create breakthroughs.

The younger generation needs to give more honor to what has come before and what has been proven. The younger generations need to understand that even in their innovation, there are proven methods that are not broken, and if they throw them off, they will never be able to get where they want to go. All innovation is built on what has come before. However, the older generations need to see and cheer on the younger generations' risk-taking and zeal. They must keep an open mind to some things that may have worked in one season but are no longer effective.

The example of the family on their journey can speak to some of this for us. Some of the proven methods on a ship will never work in the open field. While it is important to see the correlations, the generations *do* need to realize they are on different journeys in different eras. What was relevant in one season on the "sea" of what God was breathing into the church is now different in the "open field" of the "westward expansion" he is creating at this time.

Let's dive a little deeper into some of the issues we might encounter while attempting to run together as a company of pioneers.

The Will to Journey Together

I see three broad categories concerning the generations running together right now.

1. Those who want to run/work together
2. Those that have an agenda in their working together
3. Those who don't want to run together

There are different aspects and reasons for each, and I want to explore those a little bit in this next section, as I feel it's important to identify these trends if possible. I will start with the least positive, the last: "Those who don't want to run together." This category of people could have several different manifestations.

Arrogance

This can be observed in both the older and younger generations, and both need to take heed. I have observed the younger generation manifesting this by criticizing the older generation and calling them the "old wineskin." This phrase is said with a lack of wisdom because they must realize that the "new wineskin" they think they are is only "new" at this moment, and what they are criticizing was "new" not too long ago! Also, the heart of Jesus in Mark 2:22 was that both the "old" and "new" would be preserved! Throwing off what "has been" to build the new usually results in disaster. This brings with it an attitude of not only arrogance but also rebellion. Often, the younger generation is not just "working alongside" the older generation in different lanes, so to speak, but actually working directly *under* them. This means they should, in a healthy sense, be submitted to them.

Rebellion

This rebellious and arrogant attitude needs serious evaluation because it can actually open up a door to witchcraft and a spirit of divination. 1 Samuel 15:23 states that "Rebellion is as the sin of divination." This leaves a very dangerous open door for the younger generation to be influenced by or oppressed by spirits at work from the enemy. These attitudes often come from an orphan spirit or mentality as well as insecurity and competition, trying to prove something or derive affirmation that was lacking in childhood. Now, allow me to say that this doesn't always mean that what is called rebellion actually *is* rebellion because this arrogance and elitism can also be at work in the older generation.

Elitism

It is possible to reach a level of wisdom, status, and experience and slip into the mindset that you are now "untouchable" as God's anointed man or woman. Sometimes, I have seen this mindset manifest in the older generation, who criticize anyone with a dissenting idea, attitude, or perspective. They sometimes scorn the inexperience of the younger generation rather than approaching them with humility and patience.

Control

Sometimes, when the older generation sees any differing opinion as rebellion, they call it "witchcraft" or "divination" when truly it is not. If there are doors of jealousy or insecurity in the older generation of leaders, these scenarios can also happen. They can say that those "under them" are not to become "greater than them," and so they seek to hold all those who are being trained by them under their "thumb" and control and dominate them. This is just as unhealthy as the rebellion and criticisms of the younger generation and can cause an unhealthy culture to develop around them. Lastly, just as the "rebellion" of the younger generation is not always such, sometimes the "control" that the older generation can be criticized for is actually divine order.

Manipulation

Now, let's look at those with an ungodly agenda in working together.

I see this group operating from both generations and out of a spirit like Simon the sorcerer in Acts 8:9–24. Simon was, first of all, someone who, the scripture says, "claimed to be someone great." Secondly, he was known to possess "power" or to be a "power." Thirdly, when he saw the Holy Spirit being imparted, he thought about buying this power, which brought the rebuke of the apostles.

This spirit manifests in both generations whenever an agenda is involved in running together. This includes money, fame, and connections—which are not bad but become unhealthy when manipulated and misused—as well as an inflated opinion of oneself. We are to run together for the glory of God, not use one another for relevance, open doors, or connections.

I believe in multi-generational leadership, but it has to be born of God. I don't believe it's wise for a leader of the older generation to read this and think to themselves, "I have to go find someone younger to run with me," or vice-versa in the younger generations. This is ultimately a spirit of manipulation, trying to make something happen out of the flesh, trying to "buy our way" into something. Simon the sorcerer did this, and it was displeasing to the Lord. Let there be no agenda in working together other than to see the glory of God manifested in and through our lives. We must walk in the wisdom and strength of each generation running in their calling together. This is the heart of God!

Celebration

Finally, after we've touched on the negatives, let's look at those who *want to* run together. They have seen the wisdom and strength of the Lord in one another. They see the purpose in their unique manifestation of the kingdom in wisdom, strength, experience, zeal, and love. They are running together in God-formed relationships and connections, not using one another with an agenda but celebrating who each is in the Lord. They know their lane, their place, their purpose and are fulfilling that to the best of their ability. What a beautiful, powerful scenario this is!

If You Want to Go Fast

There's so much more to say on this subject, but let me leave you with one more thought. There is a famous phrase that says, "If you want to go fast, go alone...but if you want to go well, go together."

Much of what we see as it relates to trends in the Western church is a hyper-focus on building fast and big. Notoriety, influence, and "success," as the world would define it, seem to be the metric by which we evaluate what we are accomplishing in the Kingdom. We often "go it alone," and much appears to be built on personality rather than what I would consider genuine anointing. I believe this relates to the generations running together as well. It's much easier and much faster for each generation to do their own thing and build as they see fit. But is it better?

To build something well in the Kingdom requires time, thought, and intentionality. And the best scenario for us as we move into the future is for the strength of the generations to be involved in our building. We can go fast if we go alone, but that's not what God desires. It will take time, care, thought, and many hard conversations, but in the end, that building will stand the test of time. Whether you look at the

Old or New Testaments, God Himself always built like this. God is the God of Abraham, Isaac, and Jacob. He builds on the wisdom and grace from one generation to the next. Yet, in our time, it seems to be that we feel like we have to start all over in each generation! We often criticize the mistakes of those who have gone before us and built the "new wineskin" while missing the fact that each generation walks in the grace that has been apportioned to it. We don't throw away what has come before. We may need to adjust at times, and we may need to strengthen, but we always build from one generation to the next.

Let us build together, let us build well, and let us see the Spirit of the Lord and His manifestation of the spirit of Elijah break the curse off of lands and nations as we advance, arm in arm, each generation fulfilling their purpose for the cause of Christ. May the Lamb receive the reward of His suffering!

Benjamin A. Deitrick
Founder, *Ignite Ministries International*
www.igniteministries.net

About the Author

Barbara J. Yoder, a lifelong pioneer, is the apostolic founder and leader of Shekinah Christian Church as well as Breakthrough Apostolic Ministries in Ann Arbor, Michigan. She is passionate about seeing the church positioned on the cutting edge to break through to the harvest of not only individuals' lives but also cities, regions, and nations. But most of all, she longs to see the church fearlessly step into the new! Barbara resides in Ann Arbor, Michigan, and two of her favorite pastimes are traveling the world and being a first-class foodie.

Contact Information

Barbara J. Yoder
Website: www.barbarayoder.org
Email: info@shekinahchurch.org

Shekinah Christian Church
4600 Scio Church Road
Ann Arbor, MI 48103

Other Books by Barbara

Available on www.barbarayoder.com or Amazon

The Breaker Anointing: How God Breaks Open the Way to Victory

The Overcomer's Anointing: God's Plan to Use Your Darkest Hour as Your Greatest Spiritual Weapon

God's Bold Call to Women: Embrace Your God-Given Destiny with Kingdom Authority

Taking On Goliath: How to Stand Against the Spiritual Enemies in Your Life and Win

The Cry God Hears

You can also find other resources on Barbara's website, including the series *Travail: Birthing the Will of God Through Prayer.*

www.ingramcontent.com/pod-product-compliance
Lightning Source LLC
Chambersburg PA
CBHW022131080426
42734CB00006B/319